Better Homes and Gardens

Home for Dinner

170 Family-Favorite Weeknight Recipes

Better Homes and Gardens® Books
Des Moines, Iowa

Better Homes and Gardens® Books
An imprint of Meredith® Books

Home for Dinner
Editor: Jennifer Darling
Contributing Editor: Mary Major Williams
Senior Associate Design Director: Rich Michels
Designer: Jeff Harrison
Copy Chief: Catherine Hamrick
Copy and Production Editor: Terri Fredrickson
Proofreaders: Susie Kling, Sheila Mauck, Deb Smith
Electronic Production Coordinator: Paula Forest
Editorial and Design Assistants: Judy Bailey, Karen Schirm
Test Kitchen Director: Sharon Stilwell
Food Stylists: Lynn Blanchard, Jennifer Peterson, Janet Pittman
Photographers: Mike Dieter, Scott Little
Production Director: Douglas M. Johnston
Production Manager: Pam Kvitne
Assistant Prepress Manager: Marjorie J. Schenkelberg

Meredith® Books
Editor in Chief: James D. Blume
Design Director: Matt Strelecki
Managing Editor: Gregory H. Kayko
Executive Food Editor: Lisa Holderness

Director, Sales & Marketing, Retail: Michael A. Peterson
Director, Sales & Marketing, Special Markets: Rita McMullen
Director, Sales & Marketing, Home & Garden Center Channel: Ray Wolf
Director, Operations: George A. Susral

Vice President, General Manager: Jamie L. Martin

***Better Homes and Gardens®* Magazine**
Editor in Chief: Jean LemMon
Executive Food Editor: Nancy Byal

Meredith Publishing Group
President, Publishing Group: Christopher M. Little
Vice President, Consumer Marketing and Development: Hal Oringer

Meredith Corporation
Chairman and Chief Executive Officer: William T. Kerr

Chairman of the Executive Committee: E. T. Meredith III

All of us at Better Homes and Gardens® Books are dedicated to providing you with the information and ideas you need to create delicious foods. We welcome your comments and suggestions. Write to us at: Better Homes and Gardens® Books, Cookbook Editorial Department, RW-240, 1716 Locust St., Des Moines, IA 50309-3023.

If you would like to order additional copies of any of our books, check with your local bookstore.

Our seal assures you that every recipe in *Home for Dinner* has been tested in the Better Homes and Gardens® Test Kitchen. This means that each recipe is practical and reliable, and meets our high standards of taste appeal. We guarantee your satisfaction with this book for as long as you own it.

Pictured on front cover: Chicken with Peas and Potatoes (see recipe, page 56)

Dinnertime is family time! After a full day of activities, it's the perfect time of day to set aside a few minutes to be together and share your thoughts as you pass the bread and butter. Carving out a few moments of family togetherness may take a little doing, but getting a meal on the table is easy with *Better Homes and Gardens*® *Home for Dinner*.

Delight your family with hearty, meal-size soups and salads. Tempt them with home-style main dishes—they'll be back for seconds before you know it. Indulge them with new spins on popular pastas and stir-fries. Even your teens will notice the difference.

From pizzas, sandwiches, and grilled specialties to between-meal snacks and savory side dishes, we've covered the bases—sweet treats included.

So get your family together—there's no time like tonight.

Contents

Something Savory on the Side 246
Meet the supporting cast—super soups, salads, saucy pastas, and zesty vegetables that rate their own star billing on the plate.

Pass the Bread 268
Muffins, biscuits, and loaves of plenty spice up suppertime with their savory scents and satisfying flavors.

Sweet Dreams 288
Desserts galore earn you a place in glory. From down-home shortcakes and cobblers to fun and funky pizzas and the chocolate cake of your dreams, you'll find a sweet and easy finale for every meal.

Scrumptious Soups
And Salads

Beefy Vegetable Soup

8

This colorful soup starts with a less expensive meat cut but turns out a hearty soup loaded with flavor.

Trim fat from beef shanks. In a large Dutch oven or kettle combine meat, water, bouillon granules, salt, and pepper. Prepare Bouquet Garni; add to Dutch oven. Bring to boiling. Reduce heat and simmer, covered, for 2 hours.

Remove meat from soup; set aside to cool. Cut meat off bones and coarsely chop; discard bones. Skim fat from broth. Stir chopped meat, chopped tomatoes or undrained canned tomatoes, sweet potatoes, parsnips, carrot, and celery into broth.

Return to boiling. Reduce heat and simmer, covered, for 15 minutes. Stir in pea pods; simmer, covered, for 1 to 2 minutes more or until the pea pods are crisp-tender. Remove Bouquet Garni and discard.

Makes 6 servings.

Bouquet Garni: Place 4 sprigs parsley; leaves from 3 stalks celery; 2 bay leaves; 2 cloves garlic, halved; and 4 sprigs fresh thyme or 2 teaspoons dried thyme on a 10-inch-square double thickness of 100% cotton cheesecloth. Tie into a bag with a clean string.

3 **pounds beef shank crosscuts**
3 **cups water**
2 **teaspoons instant beef bouillon granules**
1½ **teaspoons salt**
¼ **teaspoon pepper**
 Bouquet Garni
2 **cups chopped, peeled tomatoes or one 16-ounce can tomatoes, cut up**
1½ **cups peeled sweet potatoes cut into ¾-inch cubes**
1 **cup parsnips cut into ½-inch pieces**
1 **cup sliced carrot**
1 **cup sliced celery**
2 **cups fresh pea pods, halved crosswise or one 6-ounce package frozen pea pods, thawed and halved crosswise**

Nutrition information per serving: 264 calories, 30 g protein, 24 g carbohydrate, 6 g fat (2 g saturated), 59 mg cholesterol, 929 mg sodium.

Rinse beans. In a large saucepan or Dutch oven combine beans and 4 cups water. Bring to boiling. Reduce heat and simmer for 2 minutes. Remove from heat. Cover and let stand 1 hour. (Or, skip the boiling water and soak beans overnight in a covered pan.) Drain and rinse beans.

In the same pan combine beans, 4 cups fresh water, beef broth, onion, garlic, and Italian seasoning. Bring to boiling. Reduce heat and simmer, covered, for 2 hours or until beans are tender.

Meanwhile, in a medium skillet cook Italian sausage until brown. Drain well on paper towels. Add cooked and drained sausage, summer squash or zucchini, undrained tomatoes, and wine or water to bean mixture. Bring to boiling. Reduce heat and simmer, covered, about 5 minutes more or until squash is tender.

Stir in spinach. Heat through. If desired, sprinkle each serving with Parmesan cheese.

Makes 4 or 5 servings.

Crockery cooker directions: Rinse beans. In a large saucepan or Dutch oven combine beans and 4 cups cold water. Boil, uncovered, for 10 minutes; drain. Prepare sausage as directed above. In a 3½- or 4-quart crockery cooker combine the drained beans, 4 cups fresh water, beef broth, onion, garlic, Italian seasoning, cooked and drained Italian sausage, squash or zucchini, undrained tomatoes, and red wine or water. Cook, covered, on low heat setting for 11 to 12 hours or until beans are tender. Just before serving, stir spinach into soup. If desired, sprinkle each serving with Parmesan cheese.

By using the crockery cooker method, you can have a dynamite dinner ready when you step in the door, even if you were on the go all day.

1¼ cups dry great northern beans

 4 cups water

1¾ cups beef broth

½ cup chopped onion

 1 clove garlic, minced

½ teaspoon dried Italian seasoning, crushed

¾ pound fresh Italian sausage links, cut into ½-inch slices

 1 medium yellow summer squash or zucchini, sliced (2 cups)

 1 14½-ounce can Italian-style tomatoes, cut up

⅓ cup dry red wine or water

½ of a 10-ounce package frozen chopped spinach, thawed and well drained

Grated Parmesan cheese (optional)

Nutrition information per serving: 563 calories, 36 g protein, 63 g carbohydrate, 19 g fat (6 g saturated), 49 mg cholesterol, 1,155 mg sodium.

Tuscan Sausage and Bean Soup

Mexican Chicken-Tortilla Soup

This soup features cilantro, a fresh herb that resembles a flattened parsley leaf. Its pungent aroma and taste, however, impart a flavor distinctive to Mexican dishes.

Place chicken broth in a large saucepan or Dutch oven; add chicken breasts. Bring to boiling. Reduce heat and simmer, covered, about 15 minutes or until chicken is tender and no longer pink. Remove chicken from broth. Let stand until cool enough to handle. Skin, bone, and finely shred chicken; set chicken aside. Discard skin and bones. Strain broth through a large sieve or colander lined with 2 layers of 100% cotton cheesecloth. Skim fat from broth and set broth aside.

In the same saucepan cook onion, cumin, and garlic in the 1 tablespoon hot oil until onion is tender but not brown. Stir in strained broth, undrained tomatoes, tomato sauce, chili peppers, cilantro or parsley, and oregano. Bring to boiling. Reduce heat and simmer, covered, for 20 minutes. Stir in shredded chicken; heat through.

Meanwhile, cut tortillas in half, then cut crosswise into ½-inch-wide strips. In a heavy medium skillet heat ¼ inch oil. Fry strips in hot oil, about half at a time, about 1 minute or until crisp and light brown. Remove with a slotted spoon; drain on paper towels.

Divide fried tortilla strips among four soup bowls. Ladle soup over tortilla strips. Sprinkle each serving with shredded cheese. Serve immediately.

Makes 4 servings.

Nutrition information per serving: 496 calories, 38 g protein, 33 g carbohydrate, 24 g fat (8 g saturated), 85 mg cholesterol, 1,658 mg sodium.

3½ cups chicken broth
 2 whole small chicken breasts
     (about 1¼ pounds total)
½ cup chopped onion
½ teaspoon ground cumin
 1 clove garlic, minced
 1 tablespoon cooking oil
 1 16-ounce can tomatoes, cut up
 1 8-ounce can tomato sauce
 1 4-ounce can whole green chili
     peppers, rinsed, seeded, and
     cut into thin bite-size strips
¼ cup snipped fresh cilantro or parsley
 1 tablespoon snipped fresh oregano or
     1 teaspoon dried oregano, crushed
 6 6-inch corn tortillas
     Cooking oil
 1 cup shredded cheddar or
     Monterey Jack cheese (4 ounces)

Chicken Soup with Lentils and Barley

Lentils and barley give this pleasing chicken soup an earthy, down-home flavor.

Rinse and drain lentils; set aside. In a large saucepan or Dutch oven cook leeks or onion, sweet red or green pepper, and garlic in margarine or butter until tender but not brown. Carefully stir in chicken broth, basil, oregano, rosemary, pepper, and the lentils. Bring to boiling. Reduce heat and simmer, covered, for 20 minutes.

Stir in the chicken or turkey, carrots, and uncooked barley. Simmer, covered, about 20 minutes more or just until carrots are tender. Stir in undrained tomatoes; heat through.

Makes 4 to 6 servings.

½ cup dry lentils

1 cup sliced leeks or chopped onion

½ cup chopped sweet red or green pepper

1 clove garlic, minced

2 tablespoons margarine or butter

5 cups chicken broth

1½ teaspoons snipped fresh basil or
   ½ teaspoon dried basil, crushed

1 teaspoon snipped fresh oregano or
   ¼ teaspoon dried oregano, crushed

¾ teaspoon snipped fresh rosemary or
   ¼ teaspoon dried rosemary, crushed

¼ teaspoon pepper

1½ cups chopped cooked chicken or turkey

1½ cups sliced carrots

½ cup quick-cooking barley

1 16-ounce can tomatoes, cut up

Nutrition information per serving: 367 calories, 28 g protein, 36 g carbohydrate, 13 g fat (3 g saturated), 51 mg cholesterol, 1,324 mg sodium.

For roux, in a large heavy saucepan or Dutch oven combine flour and oil until smooth. Cook over medium-high heat for 5 minutes, stirring constantly. Reduce heat to medium. Cook and stir about 15 minutes or until roux is dark reddish brown.

Stir in onion, celery, green pepper, garlic, black pepper, and ground red pepper. Cook over medium heat for 3 to 5 minutes or until vegetables are just crisp-tender, stirring often.

Gradually stir in hot chicken broth, chicken or turkey, sausage, okra, and bay leaves. Bring to boiling. Reduce heat and simmer, covered, about 15 minutes or until okra is tender. Discard bay leaves. Serve in bowls with rice.

If desired, serve with ¼ to ½ teaspoon filé powder to stir into each serving.

Makes 4 servings.

Filé (fee LAY) powder is ground sassafras leaves that Cajun cooks use to thicken and add a thymelike flavor to gumbos.

⅓ cup all-purpose flour

¼ cup cooking oil

½ cup chopped onion

½ cup chopped celery

½ cup chopped green pepper

 4 cloves garlic, minced

¼ teaspoon black pepper

¼ teaspoon ground red pepper

 3 cups chicken broth, heated

1½ cups chopped cooked chicken or turkey

 8 ounces andouille sausage or fully cooked
      smoked sausage links, halved
      lengthwise and cut into ½-inch slices

1½ cups sliced okra or one 10-ounce
      package frozen cut okra

 2 bay leaves

 3 cups hot cooked rice

     Filé powder (optional)

Nutrition information per serving: 614 calories, 37 g protein, 61 g carbohydrate, 24 g fat (5 g saturated), 87 mg cholesterol, 1,129 mg sodium.

Classic Chicken-Sausage Gumbo

Fish-Asparagus Bisque

Serve this thick, velvety soup with a crisp
vegetable salad and an assortment of crackers.

Thaw fish, if frozen. Cut fish into ¾-inch pieces; set aside.
In a large saucepan or Dutch oven cook leeks or onion,
mushrooms, asparagus, and garlic in margarine or butter
for 6 to 8 minutes or until vegetables are crisp-tender.
Stir in flour, thyme, and savory. Add chicken broth and
milk all at once. Cook and stir until thickened and
bubbly. Cook and stir for 1 minute more.

Add the fish. Bring to boiling. Reduce heat and simmer,
uncovered, for 3 to 5 minutes more or until fish flakes
easily with a fork. Stir in cheese.

Makes 4 servings.

½ **pound fresh or frozen cod or**
    orange roughy fillets
1 **cup sliced leeks or chopped onion**
1 **cup sliced fresh shiitake mushrooms**
    or button mushrooms
½ **pound asparagus spears, cut into**
    1-inch pieces (1 cup) or ½ of a
    10-ounce package frozen cut
    asparagus, thawed
1 **clove garlic, minced**
¼ **cup margarine or butter**
¼ **cup all-purpose flour**
1 **teaspoon snipped fresh thyme or**
    ¼ teaspoon dried thyme, crushed
1 **teaspoon snipped fresh savory or**
    ¼ teaspoon dried savory, crushed
1 **14½-ounce can chicken broth**
1¾ **cups milk**
½ **cup shredded Jarlsberg cheese or**
    Swiss cheese (2 ounces)

Nutrition information per serving: 324 calories, 22 g protein, 17 g carbohydrate,
19 g fat (6 g saturated), 43 mg cholesterol, 614 mg sodium.

In a medium saucepan combine potatoes and vegetable or chicken broth. Bring to a boil; reduce heat. Cover and simmer for 10 minutes or until potatoes are tender. Do not drain.

Meanwhile, in a large saucepan cook the green pepper, red pepper, yellow pepper, and onion in hot margarine or butter until tender but not brown. Stir in flour, salt, black pepper, and ground red pepper. Add milk all at once. Cook and stir until thickened and bubbly. Cook and stir for 1 minute more. Stir in undrained potatoes. Heat through.

To serve, ladle soup into individual bowls.

Makes 4 servings.

3 **medium potatoes, cubed (2¼ cups)**
2 **cups vegetable or chicken broth**
1 **small green pepper, chopped (½ cup)**
1 **small red sweet pepper, chopped (½ cup)**
1 **small yellow sweet pepper, chopped (½ cup)**
1 **small onion, chopped (⅓ cup)**
¼ **cup margarine or butter**
¼ **cup all-purpose flour**
¼ **teaspoon salt**
¼ **teaspoon black pepper**
⅛ **teaspoon ground red pepper**
3 **cups milk**

Nutrition information per serving: 344 calories, 12 g protein, 39 g carbohydrate, 16 g fat (5 g saturated), 14 mg cholesterol, 752 mg sodium.

Chunky Potato-Pepper Soup

In a large saucepan cook the onion in hot margarine or butter until onion is tender but not brown. Carefully add the water, eggplant, squash, brown rice, tomato paste, red wine, bouillon cubes or granules, garlic, basil, sugar, salt, and pepper. Bring to a boil; reduce heat. Cover and simmer for 30 minutes or until vegetables are very tender. Stir in cooked pasta; heat through. Lightly brush each slice of French bread with olive oil.

To serve, ladle the soup into individual bowls. Place one bread slice on top of each serving. Sprinkle with some Parmesan cheese.

Makes 4 servings.

This thick soup resembles a stew because its rich broth is chock-full of nutty brown rice and tasty vegetables.

- 2 **large onions, thinly sliced and separated into rings**
- 2 **tablespoons margarine or butter**
- 4 **cups water**
- 1 **small eggplant, peeled and chopped (4 cups)**
- 1 **small yellow summer squash or zucchini, thinly sliced (1 cup)**
- ½ **cup brown rice**
- ½ **of a 6-ounce can (⅓ cup) tomato paste**
- ¼ **cup dry red wine**
- 3 **vegetable bouillon cubes or 1 tablespoon instant beef bouillon granules**
- 1 **clove garlic, minced**
- 1½ **teaspoons dried basil, crushed**
- ½ **teaspoon sugar**
- ¼ **teaspoon salt**
- ¼ **teaspoon pepper**
- ½ **cup orzo or other small pasta, cooked and drained**
- 4 **thin slices French bread, lightly toasted Olive oil**
- ¼ **cup grated Parmesan cheese**

Nutrition information per serving: 378 calories, 11 g protein, 55 g carbohydrate, 13 g fat (3 g saturated), 5 mg cholesterol, 1,215 mg sodium.

Onion-Eggplant Soup Provençale

Prepare Tortilla Cups; set aside. Prepare Tomatillo Guacamole; chill. In a medium skillet cook ground beef and garlic until beef is brown. Drain off fat. Stir in kidney beans, corn, taco sauce, and chili powder. Bring to boiling. Reduce heat. Cover and simmer for 10 minutes. Meanwhile, in a large bowl combine lettuce, tomatoes, green pepper, cheddar cheese, and green onions.

To serve, divide the lettuce mixture among the Tortilla Cups. Top each with some of the beef mixture and the Tomatillo Guacamole.

Makes 6 servings.

Tortilla Cups: Lightly brush six 9- or 10-inch flour tortillas with a small amount of water or spray nonstick spray coating onto one side of each tortilla. Spray nonstick coating into six small oven-safe bowls or 16-ounce individual casseroles. Press tortillas, coated sides up, into bowls or casseroles. Place a ball of foil in each tortilla cup to help hold its shape. Bake in a 350° oven for 15 to 20 minutes or until light brown. Remove foil; cool. Remove Tortilla Cups from bowls. Serve immediately or store in an airtight container for up to five days.

Tomatillo Guacamole: Rinse, drain, and finely chop 4 canned tomatillos (about ⅓ cup). Or, simmer 2 husked tomatillos (about 3½ ounces) in boiling water for 10 minutes; drain and chop. In a small mixing bowl combine tomatillos; ½ of a small seeded, peeled, and chopped avocado (about ½ cup); 2 tablespoons chopped canned green chili peppers, drained; and ⅛ teaspoon garlic salt. Cover and chill for up to 24 hours. Makes about ¾ cup.

A tomatillo looks like a small green tomato but has a thin covering (that is removed before cooking). The flavor is a combination of lemon, apple, and herbs.

Tortilla Cups
Tomatillo Guacamole
8 ounces lean ground beef
3 cloves garlic, minced
1 15-ounce can dark red kidney beans, rinsed and drained
¾ cup frozen whole kernel corn
1 8-ounce jar taco sauce
1 tablespoon chili powder
8 cups torn leaf lettuce or iceberg lettuce
2 medium tomatoes, chopped
1 large green pepper, chopped
¾ cup shredded sharp cheddar cheese (3 ounces)
4 green onions, thinly sliced

Nutrition information per serving: 398 calories, 22 g protein, 49 g carbohydrate, 17 g fat (6 g saturated), 38 mg cholesterol, 801 mg sodium.

Taco Salad

Greek Salad with
Herbed Vinaigrette

No leftover lamb around? Broil some lamb chops to medium-rare. Then chill the chops completely before slicing them into thin strips.

Toss together curly endive or romaine and lettuce or spinach. Divide greens among three salad plates.

Arrange meat strips, chopped tomato, sliced cucumber, sliced radishes, and olives on greens. Sprinkle with feta cheese and green onions. Shake Herbed Vinaigrette well. Drizzle over salads. Top with anchovy fillets, if desired.

Makes 3 servings.

Herbed Vinaigrette: In a screw-top jar combine ½ cup salad oil; ⅓ cup white wine vinegar or vinegar; 1 tablespoon sugar; 2 teaspoons snipped fresh or ½ teaspoon crushed, dried thyme, oregano, or basil; ½ teaspoon paprika; ¼ teaspoon dry mustard; and ⅛ teaspoon pepper. Cover and shake well. Store any remaining dressing in the refrigerator for up to 2 weeks. Shake well before using. Makes about ¾ cup.

3 cups torn curly endive or romaine
1 ½ cups torn iceberg lettuce or spinach
6 ounces cooked lean lamb, pork, or beef, cut into bite-size strips
1 medium tomato, chopped
½ small cucumber, thinly sliced
6 radishes, sliced
2 tablespoons sliced pitted ripe olives
½ cup crumbled feta cheese (2 ounces)
2 green onions, thinly sliced
½ cup Herbed Vinaigrette
3 anchovy fillets, drained, rinsed, and patted dry (optional)

Nutrition information per serving: 431 *calories,* 20 *g protein,* 11 *g carbohydrate,* 35 *g fat (8 g saturated),* 69 *mg cholesterol,* 325 *mg sodium.*

Southwestern-Style Pork and Black Bean Salad

Serve this colorful, chili-flavored salad with an ice-cold pitcher of lemonade or limeade.

In a large mixing bowl combine black beans, pork, kidney beans, corn, green pepper, and onion.

For dressing, in a screw-top jar combine oil, vinegar, cilantro, lime juice, sugar, chili powder, cumin, salt, and garlic. Cover and shake well. Pour dressing over pork mixture. Toss lightly to coat. Cover and chill for 4 to 24 hours, stirring occasionally.

To serve, line six salad plates with leaf lettuce. Divide the pork mixture among the lettuce-lined plates. Serve with tortilla chips, if desired.

Makes 6 servings.

1   15-ounce can black beans, rinsed and drained
8   ounces cooked lean pork, cut into bite-size strips (1½ cups)
1   8-ounce can red kidney beans, rinsed and drained
1   8-ounce can whole kernel corn, drained
½   cup chopped green pepper
¼   cup chopped red onion
¼   cup salad oil
¼   cup vinegar
2   tablespoons snipped fresh cilantro
2   tablespoons lime juice
1   tablespoon sugar
1   teaspoon chili powder
1   teaspoon ground cumin
¼   teaspoon salt
1   clove garlic, minced
     Shredded leaf lettuce
     Tortilla chips (optional)

Nutrition information per serving: 303 calories, 19 g protein, 28 g carbohydrate, 16 g fat (3 g saturated), 36 mg cholesterol, 450 mg sodium.

Sprinkle both sides of chicken breasts with lemon-pepper seasoning. In a large skillet cook chicken in hot oil over medium-high heat for 5 to 6 minutes per side or until golden brown and no longer pink. Remove chicken from skillet. Cut diagonally into ½-inch-wide strips.

Meanwhile, divide mixed greens among four salad plates. Place chicken breast strips atop greens. Arrange strawberry halves, pineapple spears, avocado slices, and alfalfa sprouts on each plate. Pour Honey-Jalapeño Dressing over salads.

Makes 4 servings.

Honey-Jalapeño Dressing: In a blender container or food processor bowl combine ½ cup mayonnaise or salad dressing; 2 tablespoons honey; 1 tablespoon lime juice or lemon juice; 1 tablespoon coarse-grain brown mustard; 1 jalapeño pepper, cut up (not seeded); and ¼ teaspoon paprika. Cover and blend or process until dressing is smooth. Makes about ⅔ cup.

4 **skinless, boneless medium chicken breast halves (about 12 ounces total)**

½ **teaspoon lemon-pepper seasoning**

1 **tablespoon cooking oil**

6 **cups torn mixed greens**

3 **cups strawberries, halved**

1 **15¼-ounce can pineapple spears, drained**

1 **medium avocado, seeded, peeled, and sliced**

½ **cup alfalfa sprouts**
   Honey-Jalapeño Dressing

Nutrition information per serving: 527 calories, 21 g protein, 33 g carbohydrate, 37 g fat (5 g saturated), 61 mg cholesterol, 418 mg sodium.

Chicken and Fruit Plates with Honey-Jalapeño Dressing

Rinse wild rice in a strainer under cold running water about 1 minute. In a medium saucepan combine wild rice and chicken broth. Bring to boiling; reduce heat. Cover and simmer for 20 minutes. Stir in the long grain rice. Return to boiling; reduce heat. Cover and simmer about 20 minutes more or until wild rice and long grain rice are tender and liquid is absorbed. Cool rice slightly (about 10 minutes).

In a large mixing bowl combine warm rice, turkey or chicken, celery, and green onion.

For dressing, in a screw-top jar combine oil, tarragon, vinegar, water, mustard, salt, and pepper. Cover and shake well. Pour dressing over rice mixture. Toss lightly to coat. Cover and chill for 2 to 24 hours.

To serve, stir chopped apple into the rice mixture. Line four salad plates with lettuce leaves. Divide the rice mixture among the salad plates. Garnish with apple slices, if desired.

Makes 4 servings.

Tarragon is a spicy, sharp-flavored herb with licoricelike overtones. It's often teamed with chicken or turkey.

⅓ cup wild rice

1 14½-ounce can chicken broth

⅓ cup long grain rice

2½ cups chopped cooked turkey or chicken (12 ounces)

½ cup bias-sliced celery

¼ cup sliced green onion

¼ cup olive oil or salad oil

2 tablespoons snipped fresh tarragon or 1 teaspoon dried tarragon, crushed

2 tablespoons white wine tarragon vinegar

2 tablespoons water

1 teaspoon Dijon-style mustard

¼ teaspoon salt

¼ teaspoon cracked black pepper

1 cup chopped apple
    Red-tip leaf lettuce

1 large apple, sliced (optional)

Nutrition information per serving: 443 calories, 33 g protein, 29 g carbohydrate, 22 g fat (4 g saturated) 85 mg cholesterol, 599 mg sodium.

Tarragon Turkey Salad With Wild Rice

Chicken Noodle Salad with Peanut Dressing

Although the flavors blend upon chilling, you can serve this salad just after tossing it—with delicious results.

Cook pasta according to package directions. Drain; rinse under cold water.

In a bowl combine linguine, chicken strips, cucumber, pea pods, green onions, and tomato. Pour the Soy Peanut Dressing over noodle mixture. Toss gently to mix. Cover and chill chicken mixture for 4 to 24 hours, stirring mixture 2 or 3 times.

To serve, line 4 dinner or salad plates with the shredded napa cabbage and spinach. Top with chicken mixture. Sprinkle with peanuts.

Makes 4 servings.

Soy Peanut Dressing: In a blender container combine ¾ cup water; ¼ cup peanut butter; ¼ cup soy sauce; 2 tablespoons red wine vinegar; 2 tablespoons olive oil or salad oil; 1 tablespoon sugar; 1 tablespoon toasted sesame oil; 1 tablespoon lemon juice; 1 teaspoon grated gingerroot; 1 clove garlic, minced; and 1 teaspoon chili paste or ½ teaspoon crushed red pepper. Cover and blend until smooth. Makes about 2 cups.

6 ounces linguine or very thin spaghetti
2 cups cooked chicken cut into strips (10 ounces)
1 medium cucumber, halved lengthwise, seeded and sliced
1 cup fresh pea pods, strings removed and bias-sliced in ½-inch pieces
4 green onions, cut into ½-inch pieces
1 medium tomato, chopped
   Soy Peanut Dressing
2 cups shredded napa cabbage
2 cups shredded spinach
¼ cup chopped peanuts

Nutrition information per serving: 620 calories, 39 g protein, 53 g carbohydrate, 30 g fat (5 g saturated), 68 mg cholesterol, 1,139 mg sodium.

Seafood Salad In Pineapple Boats

If fresh pineapple isn't available, use canned pineapple chunks and serve this orange-flavored salad on lettuce-lined plates.

12 ounces fresh or frozen sea scallops
4 cups water
1 teaspoon salt
1 large pineapple (about 4½ pounds)
3 cups shredded romaine
1 cup cubed creamy Havarti cheese (4 ounces)
1 medium red sweet pepper, cut into thin, bite-size strips (1 cup)
1 8-ounce carton plain yogurt
½ teaspoon finely shredded orange peel
1 tablespoon orange juice
1 tablespoon honey
½ teaspoon vanilla
Orange peel (optional)

Thaw scallops, if frozen. Rinse and drain. Cut any large scallops in half. In a large saucepan or Dutch oven bring water and salt to boiling. Add scallops. Simmer, uncovered, for 1 to 2 minutes or until scallops are opaque, stirring occasionally. Drain and rinse under cold running water. Cover and chill scallops for 2 to 24 hours.

Use a sharp knife to cut pineapple lengthwise into quarters, crown and all. Remove the hard core from each quarter; discard. Cut out pineapple meat, leaving shells intact. Set shells aside. Remove eyes from pineapple meat. Cut pineapple into chunks, reserving 3 cups (refrigerate remaining pineapple for another use).

In a large mixing bowl combine reserved pineapple chunks, shredded romaine, Havarti cheese, and red sweet pepper. Gently stir in scallops. Spoon salad into pineapple shells.

For dressing, in a small mixing bowl stir together yogurt, finely shredded orange peel, orange juice, honey, and vanilla. Garnish dressing with additional orange peel, if desired. Serve dressing with salad.

Makes 4 servings.

Nutrition information per serving: 294 calories, 20 g protein, 26 g carbohydrate, 13 g fat (1 g saturated), 60 mg cholesterol, 371 mg sodium.

Tortellini-Caesar Salad

This main-dish version of Caesar salad features cheese-filled pasta and a cooked egg dressing in place of the traditional uncooked dressing.

For dressing, in a blender container or food processor bowl combine egg, chicken broth, anchovy fillets, oil, lemon juice, and Worcestershire sauce. Cover and blend or process until smooth. Transfer dressing to a small saucepan. Cook and stir dressing over low heat for 8 to 10 minutes or until thickened. Do not boil. Transfer to a small bowl. Cover surface with plastic wrap; chill for 2 to 24 hours.

Snap off and discard woody bases from fresh asparagus. If desired, scrape off scales. Break into 1-inch pieces. Cook asparagus, covered, in a small amount of boiling water for 4 to 8 minutes or until tender. (Or, cook frozen asparagus according to package directions.) Cook tortellini according to package directions. Drain; set aside.

To serve, rub the inside of a wooden salad bowl with the cut sides of the garlic clove. Discard garlic clove. Add romaine, asparagus, tortellini, croutons, and Parmesan cheese to salad bowl. Pour dressing over salad. Toss lightly to mix. Transfer to individual salad plates. Sprinkle pepper over each serving.

Makes 4 servings.

1   **egg**
⅓   **cup chicken broth**
3   **anchovy fillets, mashed**
3   **tablespoons olive oil or salad oil**
2   **tablespoons lemon juice**
    Few dashes white wine
        Worcestershire sauce
¾   **pound asparagus spears or one**
        10-ounce package frozen cut
        asparagus
2   **cups frozen or refrigerated cheese-**
        filled tortellini (about 7 ounces)
1   **clove garlic, halved**
10 **cups torn romaine**
½   **cup croutons**
¼   **cup finely shredded Parmesan cheese**
    Coarsely ground pepper

Nutrition information per serving: 434 calories, 21 g protein, 42 g carbohydrate, 21 g fat (4 g saturated), 97 mg cholesterol, 711 mg sodium.

Fast, Fabulous Classics

Beef and Chipotle Pinwheels

If opting for dried instead of canned chipotle peppers, use one or two and soften them in boiling water or beef broth for 10 minutes.

3 **canned chipotle chili peppers, drained**
2 **tablespoons beef broth**
2 **cloves garlic**
1 **1- to 1½-pound beef flank steak**
½ **teaspoon salt**
¼ **teaspoon ground black pepper**
¼ **cup snipped fresh chives**
1 **tablespoon margarine or butter**
1 **tablespoon all-purpose flour**
1 **tablespoon Dijon-style mustard**
½ **cup milk**
½ **cup beef broth**
1 **tablespoon snipped fresh chives**

In a blender container or food processor combine chili peppers, 2 tablespoons broth, and garlic. Cover and blend or process until smooth. Set aside.

Score steak by making shallow cuts at 1-inch intervals diagonally across the steak in a diamond pattern. Repeat on second side of meat. Using a meat mallet, pound the steak into a 12×8-inch rectangle, working from the center out to the edges. Sprinkle with salt and black pepper.

Spread chili pepper mixture over meat. Sprinkle with ¼ cup chives. Starting from the narrow end, roll up steak, jelly-roll style. Skewer with wooden toothpicks at 1-inch intervals. Cut between toothpicks into eight 1-inch slices.

Place slices, cut side down, on the unheated rack of a broiler pan. Broil 3 inches from the heat for 6 minutes. Turn and broil until desired doneness, allowing 6 to 8 minutes more for medium. Remove wooden toothpicks.

Meanwhile, for sauce, in a small saucepan melt margarine or butter. Stir in flour and mustard. Add milk and ½ cup broth. Cook and stir over medium heat until thickened and bubbly. Cook and stir 1 minute more. Stir in 1 tablespoon chives. Serve with meat.

Makes 4 servings.

Nutrition information per serving: 225 calories, 24 g protein, 5 g carbohydrate, 12 g fat (4 g saturated), 55 mg cholesterol, 730 mg sodium.

Peppery Pot Roast

Your family might dub this "pot roast with pizazz," thanks to the black pepper, red pepper, and hot pepper sauce. Any meat leftovers will make tasty sandwiches on hearty rye bread.

Trim fat from meat. Rub black pepper and red pepper over surface of meat. In a 4- to 4½-quart Dutch oven brown meat on all sides in hot oil. Drain off fat.

In a medium mixing bowl stir together vegetable juice cocktail, hot pepper sauce, garlic, bouillon granules, and mustard. Pour over meat. Bring to boiling; reduce heat. Cover and simmer for 1 hour.

Add sweet potatoes, parsnips, celery, and onion to meat mixture. Cover and simmer for 45 to 60 minutes more or until meat is tender. Add water, if necessary, during cooking. Remove meat and vegetables from pan. Keep warm.

For gravy, skim fat from pan juices; measure juices and, if necessary, add enough water to equal 1½ cups. Combine the ½ cup cold water and flour. Stir into juices; return to pan. Cook and stir until thickened and bubbly. Cook and stir 1 minute more. Season to taste with salt. Slice meat. Serve gravy with meat and vegetables.

Makes 8 to 10 servings.

1	2½- to 3-pound boneless beef chuck pot roast
1	teaspoon ground black pepper
½	teaspoon ground red pepper
2	tablespoons cooking oil
¾	cup vegetable juice cocktail
½	to 1 teaspoon bottled hot pepper sauce
4	cloves garlic, halved
1	teaspoon instant beef bouillon granules
½	teaspoon dry mustard
2	medium sweet potatoes, peeled and quartered
8	small parsnips, halved crosswise
4	stalks celery, bias-sliced into 1-inch pieces (2 cups)
1	medium onion, cut into wedges
½	cup cold water
¼	cup all-purpose flour
	Salt

Nutrition information per serving: 485 calories, 50 g protein, 33 g carbohydrate, 16 g fat (6 g saturated), 143 mg cholesterol, 372 mg sodium.

In a small saucepan combine water, ½ cup cornmeal, 1 teaspoon cumin, paprika, salt, and ¼ teaspoon black pepper. Bring just to boiling; reduce heat. Stir in margarine or butter. Cook, uncovered, over low heat for 10 minutes, stirring often. Remove from heat. Spread mixture on waxed paper into an 8-inch square. Chill while preparing meat mixture.

In a large skillet cook beef, onion, sweet pepper, and garlic over medium heat until meat is brown and onion is tender. Drain off fat. Stir in tomato sauce, corn, 1 tablespoon cornmeal, chili powder, 1 tablespoon cumin, cocoa powder, allspice, hot pepper sauce, and ¼ teaspoon black pepper. Bring to boiling; reduce heat. Simmer, uncovered, for 5 minutes.

Spoon meat mixture into a 2-quart rectangular baking dish. Cut cornmeal mixture into desired shapes, piecing together scraps, if necessary. Place on top of meat mixture.

Bake, uncovered, in a 375° oven about 30 minutes or until bubbly and cornmeal topping is light brown. Remove from oven and immediately sprinkle with cheese. Let stand 2 to 3 minutes until cheese melts.

Makes 6 servings.

Cocoa powder in a main dish pie? Yep! It helps blend the flavors of the other seasonings and gives this entrée a robust background flavor.

1¼ cups cold water
½ cup yellow cornmeal
1 teaspoon ground cumin
½ teaspoon paprika
¼ teaspoon salt
¼ teaspoon ground black pepper
2 teaspoons margarine or butter
1 pound lean ground beef
1 cup chopped onion
1 medium green sweet pepper, chopped (¾ cup)
2 cloves garlic, minced
1 15-ounce can tomato sauce
1 10-ounce package frozen whole kernel corn, thawed
1 tablespoon yellow cornmeal
1 tablespoon chili powder
1 tablespoon ground cumin
2 teaspoons unsweetened cocoa powder
½ teaspoon ground allspice
½ to 1 teaspoon bottled hot pepper sauce
¼ teaspoon ground black pepper
½ cup shredded sharp cheddar cheese (2 ounces)

Nutrition information per serving: 327 calories, 21 g protein, 31 g carbohydrate, 14 g fat (6 g saturated), 57 mg cholesterol, 678 mg sodium.

Tamale Pie

Pork Scaloppine with Mustard and Rosemary

To keep the pork warm while you prepare the sauce, place the cooked pork slices on a warm serving platter. Cover with foil and place the platter in a 300° oven.

Cut pork crosswise into ½-inch thick slices. Pound with the flat side of a meat mallet until about ⅛ inch thick. In a shallow dish combine flour, salt, and black pepper. Coat both sides of pork with seasoned flour, shaking off excess.

In a large skillet heat margarine or butter and oil over medium-high heat. Add half of the pork to skillet and cook about 2 minutes per side or until golden brown on the outside and light pink in center (juices will run clear). Remove from skillet and keep warm while cooking remaining pork. Set aside.

Reduce heat to medium. Add mushrooms, garlic, and rosemary. Cook and stir until mushrooms are just tender. Add broth, scraping up any browned bits. Bring to boiling. Boil for 5 minutes or until reduced by half. Stir in mustard, lemon peel, and lemon juice. Heat through. Spoon over pork. Garnish with lemon wedges and fresh rosemary, if desired.

Makes 4 servings.

1   pound pork tenderloin
⅓   cup all-purpose flour
¼   teaspoon salt
½   teaspoon ground black pepper
2   tablespoons margarine or butter
1   tablespoon olive oil or cooking oil
1   cup sliced fresh mushrooms
2   cloves garlic, minced
1   tablespoon snipped fresh rosemary
      or 1 teaspoon dried rosemary,
      crushed
¾   cup chicken broth
2   tablespoons Dijon-style mustard
1   teaspoon finely shredded lemon peel
1   tablespoon lemon juice
    Lemon wedges (optional)
    Fresh rosemary (optional)

Nutrition information per serving: 287 calories, 28 g protein, 10 g carbohydrate, 14 g fat (3 g saturated), 81 mg cholesterol, 594 mg sodium.

Lamb Curry

The fieriness of this dish depends on the type of curry powder you use. Imported curry powder from specialty food shops tends to be hotter than grocery store curry powder.

In a large saucepan brown half of the meat in hot oil. Remove from pan. Brown remaining meat with onion and garlic. Stir in curry powder. Cook and stir for 1 minute. Return all meat to pan.

Stir in apples, broth, coconut, raisins, brown sugar, Worcestershire sauce, and lime peel. Bring to boiling; reduce heat. Cover and simmer about 45 minutes or until meat is tender. Stir cold water into flour; stir into saucepan. Cook and stir until thickened and bubbly. Cook and stir for 1 minute more. Serve over rice. If desired, pass condiments.

Makes 4 servings.

1 pound boneless lamb, cut into
   ¾-inch cubes
1 tablespoon cooking oil
1 large onion, chopped (1 cup)
4 cloves garlic, minced
2 tablespoons curry powder
2 medium apples, peeled, cored, and
   thinly sliced
1 cup chicken broth
¼ cup shredded coconut
¼ cup raisins
2 tablespoons brown sugar
2 tablespoons Worcestershire sauce
¼ teaspoon finely shredded lime peel
¼ cup cold water
2 tablespoons all-purpose flour
2 cups hot cooked rice
   Condiments such as chopped
      peanuts, sliced bananas, pineapple
      chunks, sliced green onions, and
      chutney (optional)

Nutrition information per serving: 488 calories, 22 g protein, 57 g carbohydrate, 20 g fat (8 g saturated), 64 mg cholesterol, 320 mg sodium.

In a small bowl place dried tomatoes. Add enough boiling water to cover; soak for 10 minutes. Drain and pat dry with paper towels. Finely chop; set aside.

Rinse chicken; pat dry with paper towels. Place each breast half between 2 pieces of plastic wrap. Working from center to the edges, pound lightly with the flat side of a meat mallet to ⅛-inch thickness. Remove plastic wrap.

In a small shallow bowl combine the flour, salt, and pepper. In another small shallow bowl combine the bread crumbs, Parmesan cheese, and paprika. In another small bowl slightly beat the egg.

Cut cheddar cheese into four 3×1×½-inch pieces. Place a cheese stick on each pounded chicken breast half. Sprinkle each with some of the chopped dried tomatoes and dried herbs. Fold in the sides of each chicken breast and roll up tightly. Roll in flour mixture, egg, and then bread crumb mixture.

Arrange chicken rolls, seam side down, in a 2-quart rectangular baking dish. (To make ahead, cover and chill for 1 to 4 hours.) Drizzle chicken rolls with melted margarine or butter. Bake, uncovered, in a 350° oven for 20 to 25 minutes or until chicken is tender and no longer pink.

Makes 4 servings.

2	tablespoons dried tomatoes (not oil pack)
4	medium skinless, boneless chicken breast halves (about 12 ounces total)
2	tablespoons all-purpose flour
¼	teaspoon salt
⅛	teaspoon pepper
⅓	cup fine dry bread crumbs
2	tablespoons grated Parmesan cheese
½	teaspoon paprika
1	egg
4	ounces sharp cheddar cheese
½	to 1 teaspoon dried fines herbes or leaf sage, crushed
1	tablespoon margarine or butter, melted

Nutrition information per serving: 317 calories, 28 g protein, 11 g carbohydrate, 17 g fat (8 g saturated), 130 mg cholesterol, 953 mg sodium.

Cheese-Stuffed Chicken Rolls

Oven-Fried Chicken

For a fresh-tasting accompaniment, sprinkle sliced tomatoes with basil and marinate in a light salad dressing while the chicken is baking.

In a small bowl combine the egg and the milk. In a shallow dish combine the crackers, thyme, paprika, and pepper. Set aside.

Skin chicken. Rinse chicken; pat dry with paper towels. Dip chicken pieces, one at a time, in egg mixture, then roll in cracker mixture.

In a greased 15×10×1-inch or 13×9×2-inch baking pan arrange chicken so the pieces don't touch. Drizzle chicken pieces with melted margarine or butter.

Bake in a 375° oven for 45 to 55 minutes or until the chicken pieces are tender and no longer pink. Do not turn the chicken pieces while baking.

Makes 6 servings.

1 beaten egg
3 tablespoons milk
1 cup finely crushed saltine crackers
   (about 28)
1 teaspoon dried thyme, crushed
½ teaspoon paprika
⅛ teaspoon pepper
2½ to 3 pounds meaty chicken pieces
   (breasts, thighs, and drumsticks)
2 tablespoons margarine or butter,
   melted

Nutrition information per serving: 253 calories, 24 g protein, 10 g carbohydrate, 12 g fat (3 g saturated), 105 mg cholesterol, 296 mg sodium.

Chicken with Peas and Potatoes

Save cleanup time with this chicken meal-in-a-skillet featuring tiny red-skinned potatoes and peas in a rosemary-scented sauce.

Skin chicken, if desired. Rinse and pat dry with paper towels. Scrub potatoes. If desired, remove a narrow strip of peel from the center of each potato.

In a 12-inch skillet cook chicken in hot margarine or butter over medium heat about 15 minutes or until chicken is browned, turning to brown evenly. Add potatoes, broth, rosemary, and pepper. Bring to boiling; reduce heat. Cover and simmer for 30 minutes.

Add green onions, peas, and ¼ cup parsley to skillet. Cover and simmer about 10 minutes more or until the chicken and potatoes are tender and chicken is no longer pink. Using a slotted spoon, transfer chicken and vegetables to platter; keep warm.

Remove skillet from heat. Stir together sour cream and flour; stir into broth in skillet. Cook and stir until thickened and bubbly; cook and stir for 1 minute more. Spoon sauce over chicken and vegetables; sprinkle with additional parsley, if desired.

Makes 6 servings.

1 2½- to 3-pound cut up broiler-fryer
     chicken or 2 pounds chicken thighs
1 **pound small new potatoes, quartered**
2 **tablespoons margarine or butter**
¾ **cup chicken broth**
1 **teaspoon dried rosemary, crushed**
¼ **teaspoon pepper**
4 **green onions, thinly sliced**
1 **10-ounce package frozen peas**
¼ **cup snipped parsley**
1 **8-ounce carton dairy sour cream**
2 **tablespoons all-purpose flour**
   Snipped parsley (optional)

Nutrition information per serving: 491 calories, 34 g protein, 28 g carbohydrate, 27 g fat (10 g saturated), 106 mg cholesterol, 286 mg sodium.

Chicken and Vegetable Stew

Hearty stews, particularly this rosemary-seasoned one, are rewarding comfort food year-round.

Skin chicken. Rinse chicken; pat dry with paper towels. In a 4½-quart Dutch oven cook chicken in hot oil over medium heat for 10 to 15 minutes or until chicken is lightly browned, turning to brown evenly. Drain fat.

Add 2 cups water, potatoes, carrots, celery, fresh green beans (if using), onion, tomato paste, bay leaf, salt, and rosemary. Bring to boiling. Reduce heat; cover and simmer for 25 minutes.

Add zucchini and frozen green beans (if using). Cook, covered, for 10 to 15 minutes more or until chicken is tender and no longer pink. Discard bay leaf.

Combine ¼ cup water and flour. Add to chicken mixture. Cook and stir until thickened and bubbly. Cook and stir for 1 minute more. Sprinkle with parsley, if desired.

Makes 4 servings.

8 small chicken thighs (about
      2 pounds total)
2 tablespoons cooking oil
2 cups water
8 small new potatoes, halved
4 medium carrots, sliced into 1-inch
      pieces (2 cups)
2 stalks celery, bias-sliced into ¾-inch
      pieces (1 cup)
1 cup fresh green beans cut into 1½ inch
      pieces or frozen cut green beans
1 small onion, chopped (⅓ cup)
2 tablespoons tomato paste
1 bay leaf
¾ teaspoon salt
½ teaspoon dried rosemary, crushed
1 medium zucchini, quartered lengthwise
      and cut into ½-inch slices (1¼ cups)
¼ cup cold water
2 tablespoons all-purpose flour
   Snipped parsley (optional)

Nutrition information per serving: 424 calories, 31 g protein, 43 g carbohydrate, 15 g fat (4 g saturated), 93 mg cholesterol, 581 mg sodium.

Chicken
Ratatouille

The chicken simmers to perfection in this excellent vegetable combination that originated in the Mediterranean.

Skin chicken. Rinse chicken; pat dry with paper towels. In a 4½-quart Dutch oven cook chicken in hot oil over medium heat about 10 minutes or till chicken is lightly browned, turning to brown evenly. Remove chicken; set aside.

Add onion and garlic to drippings in Dutch oven. Cook about 5 minutes or until tender. Add tomatoes, green sweet pepper, eggplant, zucchini, bay leaf, salt, and pepper. Return chicken to Dutch oven. Bring to boiling; reduce heat. Cover and simmer about 30 minutes or until chicken is tender and no longer pink, stirring occasionally. Spoon off excess fat, if necessary.

Stir in bacon. Discard bay leaf. If desired, for a thicker sauce, transfer chicken to serving bowl; keep warm. Simmer vegetables, uncovered, for 5 to 10 minutes more. Pour sauce over chicken. Sprinkle with parsley before serving, if desired.

Makes 6 servings.

1 2½- to 3-pound cut up broiler-fryer chicken
2 tablespoons cooking oil
1 large onion, sliced
1 clove garlic, minced
2 large tomatoes, diced
1 large green sweet pepper, cut into ½-inch strips
1 small eggplant (about 1 pound), peeled and cut into 1-inch chunks
2 small zucchini, cut into ½-inch chunks
1 bay leaf
½ teaspoon salt
¼ teaspoon pepper
3 slices bacon, crisp-cooked, drained, and crumbled
  Snipped parsley (optional)

Nutrition information per serving: 339 calories, 31 g protein, 12 g carbohydrate, 19 g fat (5 g saturated), 92 mg cholesterol, 313 mg sodium.

Rinse chicken; pat dry with paper towels. In a 12-inch ovenproof skillet, cook chicken in hot oil over medium heat about 10 minutes or until chicken is lightly browned, turning to brown evenly. Remove chicken.

Add onion and garlic to skillet. Cook about 5 minutes or until onion is tender. Stir in rice. Cook and stir till rice is light brown.

Drain clams, reserving liquid; set aside. Stir cumin, salt, pepper, and saffron into skillet; add the undrained stewed tomatoes, chicken broth, water, and reserved clam liquid. Bring to boiling. Top with chicken pieces. Cover tightly and bake in a 400° oven for 15 minutes.

Stir in reserved clams, peas, shrimp, and olives. Cover and bake about 15 minutes more or till chicken is tender and no longer pink and shrimp turn pink. Let stand 5 minutes before serving. Garnish with parsley, if desired.

Makes 6 servings.

Here's a version of Spanish paella, named after the utensil in which it's cooked—a two-handled pan that doubles as a casserole.

6 small chicken breast halves or 6 medium thighs (about 2 pounds total)
2 tablespoons cooking oil
1 medium onion, chopped (½ cup)
2 cloves garlic, minced
1 cup long grain rice
1 6½-ounce can minced clams
1 teaspoon ground cumin
½ teaspoon salt
¼ teaspoon pepper
⅛ teaspoon ground saffron or ¼ teaspoon thread saffron
1 14½-ounce can stewed tomatoes
1 14½-ounce can chicken broth
¼ cup water
1 10-ounce package frozen peas
8 ounces medium raw shrimp, shelled and deveined
½ cup sliced pitted ripe olives
   Parsley sprigs (optional)

Nutrition information per serving: 437 calories, 41 g protein, 42 g carbohydrate, 12 g fat (3 g saturated), 145 mg cholesterol, 893 mg sodium.

Chicken with Saffron Rice

In a large skillet cook turkey or beef, onion, and green pepper until meat is brown and vegetables are tender. Drain fat. Cut pepperoni slices in half. Stir pepperoni, pizza sauce, mushrooms, fennel seed, oregano, and basil into meat mixture. Bring to boiling. Reduce heat and simmer, uncovered, for 10 minutes, stirring occasionally.

Meanwhile, for topping, in a small bowl combine eggs, milk, and oil. Beat with an electric mixer on medium speed for 1 minute. Add flour; beat 1 minute more or until smooth.

Grease the sides of a 13×9×2-inch baking dish; spoon meat mixture into dish. Arrange cheese slices over hot meat mixture. Pour topping over cheese, covering completely. Sprinkle with Parmesan cheese.

Bake in a 400° oven 25 to 30 minutes or until topping is puffed and golden brown. Serve immediately.

Makes 8 servings.

This saucy turkey and pepperoni mixture is topped with a layer of mozzarella cheese and a popover batter that puffs while it bakes.

1 pound ground raw turkey or ground beef

1 cup chopped onion

1 cup chopped green pepper

½ of a 3½-ounce package sliced pepperoni, halved

1 15-ounce can or one 15½-ounce jar pizza sauce

1 2-ounce can mushroom stems and pieces, drained

½ teaspoon fennel seed, crushed

½ teaspoon dried oregano, crushed

½ teaspoon dried basil, crushed

2 eggs

1 cup milk

1 tablespoon cooking oil

1 cup all-purpose flour

1 6-ounce package thinly sliced mozzarella cheese

¼ cup grated Parmesan cheese

Nutrition information per serving: 316 calories, 21 g protein, 22 g carbohydrate,16 g fat (6 g saturated), 91 mg cholesterol, 688 mg sodium.

Popover Pizza Casserole

Spinach-Topped Salmon

Salmon and asparagus are natural partners, so add some lightly steamed spears for a tasty side dish.

1½ pounds fresh or frozen salmon fillets (about ½ inch thick)

1 10-ounce package frozen chopped spinach, thawed

1 beaten egg

1 8-ounce container soft-style cream cheese with chives and onion

¼ cup grated Parmesan cheese

¾ cup herb-seasoned stuffing mix

2 tablespoons milk

2 tablespoons dry white wine or milk

¼ teaspoon garlic salt

Thaw fish, if frozen. Cut into 6 serving-size portions. Rinse fish; pat dry with paper towels. Place fish in a shallow baking dish; set aside.

For topping, drain spinach, pressing out excess liquid. In a small bowl combine egg, half of the cream cheese, and the Parmesan cheese. Stir in drained spinach and stuffing mix. Spoon one-fourth of the topping over each fillet. Bake, covered, in a 350° oven for 20 to 25 minutes or until fish flakes easily with a fork.

Meanwhile, for sauce, in a small saucepan combine remaining cream cheese, the milk, wine, and garlic salt. Cook and stir until cheese melts and mixture is smooth. Serve sauce over fish.

Makes 6 servings.

Nutrition information per serving: 310 calories, 24 g protein, 10 g carbohydrate, 18 g fat (9 g saturated), 99 mg cholesterol, 543 mg sodium.

Fish Fillets au Gratin

Mild-tasting red snapper, rockfish, and whitefish are low in fat and have a firm texture—perfect for this delicately flavored dish.

Thaw fish, if frozen. Cut fish fillets into 4 serving-size portions. Rinse fish; pat dry with paper towels. Place fish fillets in a shallow baking dish; set aside.

In a small bowl combine bread crumbs, dill, tarragon, and lemon-pepper seasoning. Stir well.

Spoon bread crumb mixture over fish. Bake, uncovered, in a 400° oven for 20 to 25 minutes or until fish flakes easily with a fork. Sprinkle with cheese; bake for 3 to 5 minutes more or until cheese melts.

Makes 4 servings.

1 **pound fresh or frozen skinless fish fillets (¾ inch thick)**
¼ **cup fine dry bread crumbs**
2 **teaspoons snipped fresh dill or**
    ½ teaspoon dried dillweed
¼ **teaspoon dried tarragon, crushed**
¼ **teaspoon lemon-pepper seasoning**
½ **cup shredded cheddar cheese**
    (2 ounces)

Nutrition information per serving: 195 calories, 28 g protein, 5 g carbohydrate, 7 g fat (3 g saturated), 57 mg cholesterol, 252 mg sodium.

Thaw fish, if frozen. Rinse fish; pat dry with paper towels. Set aside.

For stuffing, in a small bowl combine half the Swiss cheese, the almonds, chives, and 1 tablespoon of the margarine or butter. Spoon half of the stuffing onto one end of each piece of fish. Roll up fish around the stuffing. Place fish, seam side down, in a small baking dish. Sprinkle with paprika. Pour 3 tablespoons of the wine into the dish. Bake, uncovered, in a 375° oven for 15 minutes or until fish flakes easily with a fork.

Meanwhile, for sauce, in a small saucepan cook carrot in the remaining margarine or butter for 3 to 4 minutes or until tender. Stir in the flour, tarragon, salt, and white pepper; add milk all at once. Cook and stir until mixture is thickened and bubbly. Stir in remaining Swiss cheese and remaining wine.

To serve, place fish rolls atop hot cooked wild rice; top with sauce. Garnish with fresh tarragon, if desired.

Makes 2 servings.

 2 **4-ounce fresh or frozen flounder or sole fillets (¼ to ½ inch thick)**
 ½ **cup shredded Swiss cheese (2 ounces)**
 2 **tablespoons chopped almonds**
 1 **tablespoon snipped chives**
 2 **tablespoons margarine or butter, softened**
    Paprika
 ¼ **cup dry white wine**
 ¼ **cup shredded carrot**
 2 **teaspoons all-purpose flour**
 ⅛ **teaspoon dried tarragon, crushed**
    Dash salt
    Dash white pepper
 ½ **cup milk**
 1 **cup hot cooked wild rice**
    Fresh tarragon (optional)

Nutrition information per serving: 542 calories, 34 g protein, 27 g carbohydrate, 31 g fat (10 g saturated), 84 mg cholesterol, 465 mg sodium.

Almond-Stuffed Flounder with Creamy Tarragon Sauce

Thaw fish, if frozen. Rinse fish; pat dry with paper towels. Set aside.

Cut each carrot into 4 long strips (8 strips total). In a medium saucepan cook carrots, mushrooms, and celery in a small amount of boiling water for 5 minutes or just until tender. Drain, separating carrots from mushrooms and celery. Set the vegetables aside.

Combine the yogurt and mustard; set aside ⅓ cup of the mustard mixture. Brush the remaining mustard mixture over one side of each fillet. Lay one-fourth of the red and green pepper strips and two carrot strips crosswise on mustard side of each fillet. Starting from a short end, roll up each fillet around the vegetables.

Arrange fish rolls, seam side down, in a 9×9×2-inch baking pan. Brush with melted margarine or butter. Bake, uncovered, in a 400° oven for 15 to 20 minutes or until fish flakes easily with a fork.

Meanwhile, for sauce, in a small saucepan stir flour into reserved ⅓ cup mustard mixture; stir in milk. Add cooked mushrooms and celery. Cook and stir over medium heat until mixture is thickened and bubbly; cook and stir for 1 minute more. Remove from heat.

Transfer fish rolls to dinner plates. Spoon sauce over fish. Garnish with fresh dill and halved lemon wedges, if desired.

Makes 4 servings.

If the fish fillets are small, overlap two or three to make one four-ounce serving. If they're too large, cut them into serving-size portions.

4 fresh or frozen croaker, mullet, flounder, whiting, turbot, or pollack fillets (1 pound)
2 medium carrots
1 cup sliced fresh mushrooms
⅓ cup sliced celery
½ cup plain yogurt
1 to 2 tablespoons Dijon-style mustard
½ medium red sweet pepper, thinly sliced into strips (½ cup)
½ medium green pepper, thinly sliced into strips (½ cup)
1 tablespoon margarine or butter, melted
1 teaspoon all-purpose flour
3 tablespoons milk
   Fresh dill (optional)
   Lemon wedges, halved (optional)

Nutrition information per serving: 361 calories, 26 g protein, 19 g carbohydrate, 20 g fat (5 g saturated), 107 mg cholesterol, 630 mg sodium.

Fish à la Diable

Deep-Dish Tuna Pie

A convenient, off-the-shelf piecrust mix makes a flaky top that looks and tastes as if you made it from scratch.

½ of an 11-ounce package piecrust mix (1⅓ cups)
1 large onion, chopped (1 cup)
1 medium potato, peeled and diced (about 1 cup)
1 10¾-ounce can condensed cream of mushroom soup
⅓ cup milk
⅓ cup grated Parmesan cheese
1 tablespoon lemon juice
¾ teaspoon dried dillweed
¼ teaspoon pepper
1 16-ounce package frozen mixed vegetables
1 9¼-ounce can tuna, drained and broken into chunks
1 beaten egg

Prepare piecrust mix according to package directions but do not roll out. Cover dough; set aside.

In a large skillet cook onion and potato in a small amount of water, covered, about 7 minutes or until tender. Drain off liquid. Stir in soup, milk, Parmesan cheese, lemon juice, dillweed, and pepper. Cook and stir until mixture is bubbly. Gently stir in frozen mixed vegetables and tuna. Spoon mixture into an ungreased 2-quart casserole.

On a lightly floured surface roll pastry into a circle 2 inches larger than the diameter of the top of the casserole and about ⅛ inch thick. Make 1-inch slits near the center of the pastry. Center pastry over top of casserole, allowing ends to hang over edge. Trim pastry ½ inch beyond edge of casserole. Turn pastry under; flute to the casserole edge, pressing gently. Brush pastry with beaten egg.

Bake in a 400° oven for 40 to 45 minutes or until crust is golden brown. Serve immediately.

Makes 6 servings.

Nutrition information per serving: 386 calories, 21 g protein, 35 g carbohydrate, 18 g fat (5 g saturated), 49 mg cholesterol, 893 mg sodium.

Thaw scallops and spinach, if frozen. Rinse scallops and drain. Cut any large scallops in half; set aside.

Drain spinach well; divide evenly among 4 coquille shells. Arrange scallops in a single layer on spinach. Broil 3 to 4 inches from the heat for 6 to 7 minutes or until scallops are opaque.

Meanwhile, for sauce, in a small saucepan cook the ¼ cup carrot and green onion in 2 tablespoons margarine or butter. Cook for 1 minute. Stir in flour, tarragon, and pepper. Add broth and half-and-half, light cream, or milk all at once. Cook and stir until mixture is thickened and bubbly. Cook and stir for 1 minute more. Spoon sauce over the scallops in shells.

In a small mixing bowl combine bread crumbs, Parmesan cheese, and the 2 tablespoons melted margarine or butter; sprinkle over scallops and sauce in shells. Return to broiler; broil about 2 minutes or until crumbs are golden. Sprinkle with additional shredded carrot, if desired.

Makes 4 servings.

If you don't have coquille shells, use four individual au gratin dishes. Bake the scallops in a 450° oven 10 to 12 minutes or until opaque. Top with the sauce, sprinkle with the crumbs, and bake until golden.

1   **pound fresh or frozen scallops**
1   **10-ounce package frozen chopped spinach**
¼   **cup finely shredded carrot**
2   **green onions, thinly sliced (about 2 tablespoons)**
2   **tablespoons margarine or butter**
3   **tablespoons all-purpose flour**
¼   **teaspoon dried tarragon, crushed**
    Dash pepper
1   **cup chicken or vegetable broth**
⅓   **cup half-and-half, light cream, or milk**
¼   **cup fine dry bread crumbs**
2   **tablespoons grated Parmesan cheese**
2   **tablespoons margarine or butter, melted**
    Shredded carrot (optional)

Nutrition information per serving: 286 calories, 21 g protein, 15 g carbohydrate, 16 g fat (4 g saturated), 44 mg cholesterol, 656 mg sodium.

Sea Shell Scallops

Thaw fish, if frozen. Flake coarsely; set aside.

Wrap corn tortillas in foil; place in a 350° oven for 10 to 15 minutes or until softened.

Meanwhile, for sauce, in a medium saucepan cook red onion, garlic, coriander, and pepper in margarine or butter until onion is tender. In a medium bowl stir flour into sour cream. Add broth; stir until combined. Add sour cream mixture to onion mixture. Stir in jalapeño or chili peppers. Cook and stir over medium heat till mixture is slightly thickened and bubbly. Remove from heat. Add half of the cheese; stir until melted.

For filling, stir ½ cup of the sauce into flaked fish. Place about ¼ cup of the filling on each tortilla; roll up. Arrange tortilla rolls, seam side down, in a lightly greased 2-quart rectangular baking dish. Top with remaining sauce. Bake, covered, in a 350° oven for 30 to 35 minutes or until heated through.

Sprinkle with remaining cheese. Bake, uncovered, about 5 minutes more or until cheese melts. Let stand 10 minutes before serving. If desired, garnish with tomatoes, red or green onion, and cilantro.

Makes 4 servings.

Seafood-flavored fish (surimi) is made by processing and reforming minced fish to look like shellfish. Less expensive than crab or lobster, it's also lower in cholesterol.

12 ounces frozen, crab-flavored, salad-style fish

8 6¼-inch corn tortillas

1 medium red onion, finely chopped (½ cup)

2 cloves garlic, minced

1 teaspoon ground coriander

¼ teaspoon pepper

2 tablespoons margarine or butter

3 tablespoons all-purpose flour

1 8-ounce carton dairy sour cream

1 14½-ounce can chicken broth

1 or 2 canned jalapeño peppers, rinsed, seeded, and chopped, or one 4-ounce can diced green chili peppers, drained

1 cup shredded Monterey Jack cheese (4 ounces)

Chopped tomatoes (optional)

Chopped red onion or sliced green onions (optional)

Fresh cilantro (optional)

Nutrition information per serving: 550 calories, 26 g protein, 44 g carbohydrate, 30 g fat (15 g saturated), 68 mg cholesterol, 1,461 mg sodium.

Seafood Enchiladas

Florida Crab
Cakes

Maryland is renowned for crab cakes, but these golden specialties are winners in the Sunshine State.

1	6-ounce package frozen crabmeat or one 6-ounce can crabmeat, drained, flaked and cartilage removed (about 1½ cups)
1	egg, slightly beaten
½	cup fine dry bread crumbs
2	green onions, finely chopped (2 tablespoons)
2	tablespoons mayonnaise or salad dressing
1	tablespoon snipped parsley
2	teaspoons snipped fresh thyme or ½ teaspoon dried thyme, crushed
2	teaspoons Dijon-style or Creole mustard
½	teaspoon white wine Worcestershire sauce
⅛	teaspoon salt
¼	cup cornmeal
2	tablespoons cooking oil
	Salad greens (optional)
	Tartar sauce (optional)
	Lemon wedges (optional)

Thaw crab, if frozen; set aside.

In a medium bowl combine egg, ¼ cup of the fine dry bread crumbs, green onions, mayonnaise or salad dressing, parsley, thyme, mustard, Worcestershire sauce, and salt. Add crab; mix well. Shape crab mixture into four ¾-inch-thick patties.

In a small bowl combine remaining fine dry bread crumbs and cornmeal. Coat patties with cornmeal mixture.

In a large skillet heat the cooking oil; add crab cakes. Cook over medium heat about 3 minutes on each side or until crab cakes are golden and heated through, adding additional oil, if necessary. Serve crab cakes on a bed of salad greens and top with tartar sauce, if desired. Garnish with lemon wedges, if desired.

Makes 4 servings.

Tartar Sauce: In a small bowl stir together 1 cup mayonnaise or salad dressing, ¼ cup finely chopped dill pickle or sweet pickle relish, 1 tablespoon sliced green onion, 1 tablespoon snipped parsley, 1 tablespoon diced pimiento, and 1 teaspoon lemon juice. Cover and chill until serving. Makes 1 cup.

Nutrition information per serving: 259 calories, 13 g protein, 17 g carbohydrate, 15 g fat (2 g saturated), 100 mg cholesterol, 401 mg sodium.

Thaw shrimp, if frozen; set aside.

In a medium saucepan melt margarine or butter. Stir in flour, salt, and red pepper. Add milk all at once. Cook and stir until mixture is thickened and bubbly. Cook and stir for 1 minute more.

Stir about half of the hot mixture into the egg yolk. Return all of the egg mixture to the saucepan. Cook and stir just until mixture bubbles. Reduce heat. Cook and stir for 2 minutes more.

Stir in shrimp, crabmeat, lobster, and Madeira or sherry; heat through. Spoon into patty shells or serve over hot cooked rice or pasta. If desired, garnish with sage.

Makes 4 servings.

4 **ounces frozen, peeled, cooked shrimp (about ½ cup)**
2 **tablespoons margarine or butter**
2 **tablespoons all-purpose flour**
¼ **teaspoon salt**
 Dash ground red pepper
1¾ **cups milk**
1 **egg yolk, beaten**
1 **6- or 7-ounce can crabmeat, drained, flaked, and cartilage removed, or 7 ounces cooked crabmeat (about ½ cups)**
3 **ounces cooked lobster, cut into bite-size pieces (about 1 cup)**
3 **tablespoons Madeira or dry sherry**
4 **baked patty shells or 2 cups hot cooked rice or pasta**
 Fresh sage (optional)

Nutrition information per serving: 453 calories, 26 g protein, 26 g carbohydrate, 26 g fat (3 g saturated), 182 mg cholesterol, 833 mg sodium.

Crab, Lobster, and Shrimp Newburg

Double Corn Tortilla Casserole

The double dose of corn comes from corn tortillas and whole kernel corn. Serve this tangy home-style dish with your favorite salsa or picante sauce.

8 corn tortillas
1½ cups shredded Monterey Jack cheese
    (6 ounces)
1 cup frozen whole kernel corn
4 green onions, sliced (½ cup)
2 eggs
1 cup buttermilk
1 4-ounce can diced green chili
    peppers

Grease a 2-quart square baking dish. Tear tortillas into bite-size pieces. Arrange half of the tortillas in baking dish. Top with half of the cheese, half of the corn, and half of the green onions. Repeat layering with remaining tortillas, cheese, corn, and onions.

Stir together eggs, buttermilk, and chili peppers. Gently pour over tortilla mixture. Bake, uncovered, in a 325° oven about 30 minutes or until a knife inserted near the center comes out clean. Serve warm.

Makes 4 servings.

Nutrition information per serving: 388 calories, 21 g protein, 37 g carbohydrate, 18 g fat (9 g saturated), 146 mg cholesterol, 564 mg sodium.

Crispy Eggplant with Spicy Tomato-Feta Cheese Sauce

For mild cheese flavor, sprinkle feta cheese over the spaghetti sauce. For more robust flavor, use blue cheese.

1 medium eggplant (about 1 pound), peeled and thinly sliced

Salt

2 eggs

2 tablespoons milk

½ cup grated Parmesan cheese

½ cup toasted wheat germ

1 teaspoon dried basil, crushed

¼ teaspoon pepper

2 cups meatless spaghetti sauce

¼ to ½ teaspoon ground red pepper

1 cup crumbled feta or blue cheese

Fresh snipped basil or parsley (optional)

Place eggplant slices on a baking sheet; lightly salt. Let stand for 10 minutes. Pat dry with paper towels.

In a shallow bowl combine the eggs and milk. In another shallow bowl stir together the Parmesan cheese, wheat germ, basil, and pepper. Dip the eggplant slices in egg mixture, then in wheat germ mixture, turning to coat both sides. Place the coated slices in a single layer on a greased baking sheet. Bake, uncovered, in a 400° oven for 15 to 20 minutes or until the eggplant is crisp on the outside and tender on the inside.

Meanwhile, for sauce, in a medium saucepan combine the spaghetti sauce and ground red pepper. Cook over medium heat until heated through.

To serve, place several slices of eggplant on individual plates. Spoon tomato sauce over eggplant. Sprinkle with feta or blue cheese and, if desired, fresh basil or parsley.

Makes 4 servings.

Nutrition information per serving: 388 calories, 20 g protein, 35 g carbohydrate, 20 g fat (9 g saturated), 142 mg cholesterol, 1,471 mg sodium.

In a Dutch oven cook the green pepper, yellow pepper, celery, onion, red onion, and garlic in hot oil until onion is tender but not brown.

Rinse lentils. Add lentils, vegetable or chicken broth, and saffron or turmeric to the pepper mixture. Bring to a boil; reduce heat. Cover and simmer for 20 to 30 minutes or until lentils are tender and liquid is absorbed. Stir in tomatoes, peas, stuffed olives, ripe olives, and cilantro or parsley. Heat through. Season to taste before serving.

Makes 4 servings.

Traditional Spanish paella contains chicken, seafood, rice, and vegetables. This hearty version uses lentils and a colorful medley of vegetables and seasonings.

1 **medium green pepper, chopped (1 cup)**
1 **medium yellow sweet pepper, chopped (1 cup)**
2 **stalks celery, sliced (1 cup)**
1 **medium onion, chopped (½ cup)**
1 **medium red onion, chopped (½ cup)**
4 **cloves garlic, minced**
2 **tablespoons olive oil or cooking oil**
1 **cup lentils**
1¾ **cups vegetable or chicken broth**
⅛ **teaspoon powdered saffron or ½ teaspoon ground turmeric**
2 **medium tomatoes, seeded and chopped (1 cup)**
1 **cup frozen peas, thawed**
⅓ **cup pimiento-stuffed olives**
⅓ **cup pitted ripe olives**
¼ **cup snipped cilantro or parsley**

Nutrition information per serving: 306 calories, 16 g protein, 46 g carbohydrate, 10 g fat (1g saturated), 0 mg cholesterol, 1,034 mg sodium.

Vegetarian Lentil Paella

Wheat Berry-Watercress Quiche

Watercress gives peppery bite while wheat berries and egg whites make a healthy addition. If necessary, substitute ⅔ cup cooked wild rice for the wheat berries.

Line the bottom of pastry shell with a double thickness of foil. Bake in a 450° oven for 8 minutes. Remove foil; bake 4 to 5 minutes more or until set and dry. Set aside. Reduce oven temperature to 325°.

In a bowl stir together eggs, egg whites, milk, mustard, watercress leaves, green onion, salt, and pepper.

Sprinkle cooked wheat berries in the bottom of pastry shell. Top with shredded Swiss cheese. Slowly pour egg mixture over wheat berry mixture. Bake in a 325° oven about 50 minutes or until a knife inserted near the center comes out clean. If necessary, cover edge of crust with foil to prevent overbrowning. Let stand for 10 minutes.

*Note: To cook wheat berries, in a small saucepan bring 1 cup water and ⅓ cup uncooked wheat berries to a boil; reduce heat. Cover and simmer for 1 hour. Drain well on paper towels.

Makes 6 servings.

1 9-inch unbaked pastry shell
2 eggs
2 egg whites
1½ cups milk
1 tablespoon Dijon-style mustard
½ cup coarsely chopped watercress leaves
¼ cup sliced green onion
¼ teaspoon salt
¼ teaspoon pepper
⅔ cup cooked wheat berries*
1½ cups shredded Swiss cheese (6 ounces)

Nutrition information per serving: 433 calories, 19 g protein, 39 g carbohydrate, 23 g fat (9 g saturated), 101 mg cholesterol, 387 mg sodium.

In a hurry? Prepare packaged instant mashed potatoes (enough for four servings) instead of potatoes and stir in the garlic mixture.

Peel and quarter potatoes. Cook, covered, in a small amount of boiling lightly salted water for 20 to 25 minutes or till tender. Drain. Mash with a potato masher or beat with an electric mixer on low speed. In a small saucepan cook garlic and dried basil in margarine or butter for 15 seconds. Add to mashed potatoes along with salt. Gradually beat in enough milk to make light and fluffy. Set aside.

For filling, in a medium saucepan cook onion and carrot in hot oil till onion is tender but not brown. Stir in kidney beans, tomatoes, frozen vegetables, tomato sauce, Worcestershire sauce, and sugar. Heat till bubbly.

Transfer vegetable mixture to an 8×8×2-inch square baking pan. Drop mashed potatoes in 4 mounds over vegetable mixture. Sprinkle with cheddar cheese and, if desired, paprika. Bake, uncovered, in a 375° oven for 25 to 30 minutes or until heated through and cheese begins to brown.

Makes 4 servings.

3 **small potatoes (¾ pound)**
2 **cloves garlic, minced**
½ **teaspoon dried basil, crushed**
2 **tablespoons margarine or butter**
¼ **teaspoon salt**
2 **to 4 tablespoons milk**
1 **medium onion, chopped (½ cup)**
1 **medium carrot, sliced (½ cup)**
1 **tablespoon cooking oil**
1 **15-ounce can kidney beans, rinsed and drained**
1 **14½-ounce can whole tomatoes, drained and cut up**
1 **10-ounce package frozen whole kernel corn or mixed vegetables**
1 **8-ounce can tomato sauce**
1 **teaspoon Worcestershire sauce**
½ **teaspoon sugar**
1 **cup shredded cheddar cheese (4 ounces)**
   Paprika (optional)

Nutrition information per serving: 456 calories, 20 g protein, 60 g carbohydrate, 19 g fat (8 g saturated), 31 mg cholesterol, 1,130 mg sodium.

Savory Shepherd's Pie

Spaghetti Squash Italiano

Save time! Prick the whole squash with a sharp knife and place in a microwave-safe dish. Cook, uncovered, on high for 15 to 20 minutes or until tender. Let stand for 5 minutes.

Halve squash lengthwise and remove the seeds. Prick skin all over. Place halves, cut side down, in a 3-quart rectangular baking dish. Cover and bake in a 350° oven for 60 to 70 minutes or until tender. Using a fork, separate the squash pulp into strands, leaving strands in shell. Sprinkle one-fourth of the mozzarella cheese in each shell; toss lightly. Press mixture up the sides of the shell.

Meanwhile, in a bowl combine tomatoes, green onions, nuts, basil or parsley, oil, and garlic. Spoon one-fourth of the tomato mixture into each shell. Sprinkle with Parmesan cheese. Return to baking dish. Return to oven and bake, uncovered, about 20 minutes or until filling is heated through.

Makes 4 servings.

2 **small spaghetti squash (1¼ to 1½ pounds)**
4 **ounces mozzarella cheese, cut into small cubes (1 cup)**
3 **medium tomatoes, seeded and chopped (1½ cups)**
4 **green onions, sliced (½ cup)**
½ **cup pine nuts or coarsely chopped walnuts, toasted**
¼ **cup snipped fresh basil or parsley**
1 **tablespoon olive oil or cooking oil**
2 **cloves garlic, minced**
2 **tablespoons grated Parmesan cheese**

Nutrition information per serving: 304 calories, 15 g protein, 23 g carbohydrate, 20 g fat (6 g saturated), 18 mg cholesterol, 237 mg sodium.

Pasta Pleasers

Taco
Spaghetti

Feel like Mexican cuisine tonight? This combination of pasta, salsa, ground beef, and cheese captures south-of-the-border flavors.

Cook pasta according to package directions. Drain pasta; rinse with cold water. Drain again.

In a 12-inch skillet cook ground beef or turkey and onion till meat is brown. Drain fat. Stir in water and taco seasoning. Bring to boiling; reduce heat. Simmer, uncovered, for 2 minutes, stirring occasionally. Stir in cooked pasta, corn, olives, half of the shredded cheese, salsa, and chili peppers.

Transfer mixture to a lightly greased 2-quart round casserole. Cover and bake in a 350° oven for 15 to 20 minutes or until heated through. Sprinkle with remaining cheese.

Serve with shredded lettuce, tortilla chips, and tomato wedges. If desired, top with sour cream.

Makes 6 servings.

5 ounces packaged dried spaghetti, linguine, or fettuccine, broken
1 pound ground beef or ground raw turkey
1 large onion, chopped (1 cup)
¾ cup water
½ of a 1¼-ounce envelope taco seasoning mix (2 tablespoons)
1 11-ounce can whole kernel corn with sweet peppers, drained
1 cup sliced pitted ripe olives
1 cup shredded Cojack or cheddar cheese (4 ounces)
½ cup salsa
1 4-ounce can diced green chili peppers, drained
6 cups shredded lettuce
1 cup broken tortilla chips
1 medium tomato, cut into thin wedges
   Dairy sour cream (optional)

Nutrition information per serving: 438 calories, 26 g protein, 42 g carbohydrate, 21 g fat (8 g saturated), 66 mg cholesterol, 949 mg sodium.

Cook the manicotti shells according to package directions. Drain shells; rinse with cold water. Drain again.

For sauce, in a medium saucepan cook the onion and garlic in the margarine or butter until onion is tender. Stir in flour, bouillon granules, paprika, red pepper, and black pepper. Add milk all at once. Cook and stir till thickened and bubbly. Cook and stir for 1 minute more. Gradually add cheese, stirring until melted. Remove from heat.

In a large skillet cook the ground beef or pork until brown. Drain fat. Stir in peas, walnuts, 2 tablespoons pimiento, and 1 cup of the sauce. Fill each manicotti with about ¼ cup of the meat mixture. Arrange manicotti in six individual au gratin dishes or in a 3-quart rectangular baking dish. Pour the remaining sauce over the filled manicotti. Cover manicotti with foil.

Bake in a 350° oven about 20 minutes for individual dishes or about 35 minutes for the baking dish or until heated through. If desired, sprinkle with sliced green onion and additional diced pimiento.

Makes 6 servings.

12 **packaged dried manicotti shells**
1 **medium onion, chopped (½ cup)**
1 **clove garlic, minced**
3 **tablespoons margarine or butter**
3 **tablespoons all-purpose flour**
1½ **teaspoons instant chicken bouillon granules**
½ **teaspoon paprika**
¼ **to ½ teaspoon ground red pepper**
¼ **to ½ teaspoon ground black pepper**
2¼ **cups milk**
1 **cup shredded process Swiss cheese (4 ounces)**
12 **ounces ground beef or pork**
1 **cup frozen peas**
¾ **cup chopped walnuts**
2 **tablespoons diced pimiento**
  Sliced green onion (optional)
  Diced pimiento (optional)

Nutrition information per serving: 515 calories, 26 g protein, 40 g carbohydrate, 28 g fat (8 g saturated), 58 mg cholesterol, 634 mg sodium.

Stuffed Manicotti with Peppery Cheese Sauce

Baked Mostaccioli With Meat Sauce

Bake these single-serving casseroles, topped with lots of melted cheese, for a hot and satisfying supper.

Cook pasta according to package directions. Drain pasta; rinse with cold water. Drain again.

In a blender container or food processor bowl combine undrained tomatoes, tomato paste, wine or water, sugar, oregano, thyme, and pepper. Cover and blend or process till smooth. Set aside.

In a large skillet cook ground beef, onion, and garlic until meat is brown. Drain fat. Stir in tomato mixture. Bring to boiling; reduce heat. Cover and simmer for 10 minutes. Stir in pasta and olives.

Divide the pasta mixture among six 10-ounce casseroles. Bake in a 375° oven for 15 minutes. (Or, spoon all of the pasta mixture into a 2-quart casserole and bake for 30 minutes.) Sprinkle with mozzarella cheese. Bake 5 minutes more or until heated through.

Makes 6 servings.

8 ounces packaged dried mostaccioli or cavatelli
1 16-ounce can plum tomatoes
½ of a 6-ounce can (⅓ cup) tomato paste
¼ cup dry red wine or water
½ teaspoon sugar
½ teaspoon dried oregano, crushed
½ teaspoon dried thyme, crushed
¼ teaspoon pepper
1 pound ground beef
1 medium onion, chopped (½ cup)
1 clove garlic, minced
½ cup sliced pimiento-stuffed green olives
1 cup shredded mozzarella cheese (4 ounces)

Nutrition information per serving: 367 calories, 25 g protein, 38 g carbohydrate, 13 g fat (5 g saturated), 58 mg cholesterol, 572 mg sodium.

Fusilli with Creamy Tomato And Meat Sauce

Whipping cream enriches this herbed tomato and meat sauce. Serve it over your favorite pasta strands.

12 ounces ground beef or ground raw turkey

1 large onion, chopped (1 cup)

2 cloves garlic, minced

2 14-ounce cans peeled Italian-style tomatoes, cut up

1 teaspoon dried Italian seasoning, crushed

½ teaspoon sugar

¼ teaspoon salt

⅛ teaspoon pepper

8 ounces packaged dried fusilli, vermicelli, or spaghetti

½ cup whipping cream

2 tablespoons snipped parsley
   Fresh rosemary sprigs (optional)

For sauce, in a large saucepan cook beef or turkey, onion, and garlic until meat is brown. Drain fat. Stir in the undrained tomatoes, Italian seasoning, sugar, salt, and pepper. Bring to boiling; reduce heat. Simmer, uncovered, about 40 minutes or until most of liquid has evaporated, stirring occasionally.

Meanwhile, cook pasta according to package directions. Drain; keep warm.

Gradually stir the whipping cream into the sauce. Heat through, stirring constantly. Remove from heat. Stir in the parsley.

Arrange the pasta on individual plates or a large platter. Spoon the sauce over the pasta. If desired, garnish with fresh rosemary sprigs.

Makes 4 servings.

Nutrition information per serving: 523 calories, 26 g protein, 59 g carbohydrate, 21 g fat (10 g saturated), 94 mg cholesterol, 534 mg sodium.

In a Dutch oven or large saucepan cook pasta and carrots in a large amount of boiling salted water for 7 minutes, stirring occasionally. Add broccoli flowerets. Return to boiling and cook for 3 to 5 minutes more or until pasta is tender but slightly firm and vegetables are crisp-tender. Drain pasta and vegetables; keep warm.

Meanwhile, for sauce, cook mushrooms in margarine or butter until tender. Stir in flour, parsley, and basil. Add milk all at once. Cook and stir till thickened and bubbly. Add ham and cheddar cheese, stirring until cheese melts. Pour sauce over pasta and vegetables; toss to coat.

Makes 4 servings.

Make dinner easy on yourself. Buy the cut-up vegetables from your grocery store's salad bar and pick up a package of shredded cheese.

6 ounces packaged dried spinach and/or plain linguine

2 medium carrots, cut into ½-inch pieces (1 cup)

1 cup broccoli flowerets

1 cup sliced fresh mushrooms

2 tablespoons margarine or butter

2 tablespoons all-purpose flour

1 tablespoon snipped parsley

½ teaspoon dried basil, crushed

1¼ cups milk

6 ounces sliced fully cooked ham, cut into bite-size strips

½ cup shredded cheddar cheese (2 ounces)

Nutrition information per serving: 417 calories, 23 g protein, 47 g carbohydrate, 15 g fat (6 g saturated), 33 mg cholesterol, 711 mg sodium.

Ham and Pasta with Mushroom-Cheese Sauce

Ham, Spinach, and Mostaccioli Casserole

Just before serving, be sure to give the casserole a good stir to distribute the rich and creamy sauce.

Cook pasta according to package directions. Drain pasta; rinse with cold water. Drain again.

In a large saucepan melt margarine or butter. Add onion or leeks and garlic. Cover and cook about 5 minutes or until onions are tender, stirring occasionally. Stir in flour, thyme, and pepper. Add half-and-half, light cream, or milk and the chicken broth all at once. Cook and stir until thickened and bubbly. Cook and stir for 1 minute more. Stir in pasta, ham, and spinach. Spoon mixture into a 3-quart casserole.

Cover and bake in a 350° oven for 30 to 35 minutes or until heated through. Let stand 5 minutes. Stir gently before serving.

Makes 6 servings.

8 ounces packaged dried mostaccioli, cut ziti, or elbow macaroni

3 tablespoons margarine or butter

3 medium onions, cut into thin wedges, or 5 medium leeks, sliced

2 cloves garlic, minced

¼ cup all-purpose flour

½ teaspoon dried thyme, crushed

⅛ teaspoon pepper

1½ cups half-and-half, light cream, or milk

1½ cups chicken broth

1½ cups cubed fully cooked ham

1 10-ounce package frozen chopped spinach, thawed and drained

Nutrition information per serving: 388 calories, 18 g protein, 44 g carbohydrate, 16 g fat (6 g saturated), 42 mg cholesterol, 719 mg sodium.

Cook fettuccine according to package directions. Drain well.

Meanwhile, in a 12-inch skillet cook mushrooms and green onions in margarine or butter about 5 minutes or until vegetables are tender. Stir in flour, salt, pepper, and nutmeg. Add milk; cook and stir until thickened and bubbly. Cook and stir for 1 minute more. Add half of the Parmesan cheese and the sherry; heat until cheese is melted.

Add fettuccine, chicken, and ripe olives to skillet. Toss lightly to coat. Sprinkle with remaining Parmesan and, if desired, chives. Serve with lemon wedges, if desired.

Makes 4 servings.

Although packaged grated Parmesan can be used here, freshly grated or shredded cheese intensifies the flavor.

- 6 **ounces spinach fettuccine or plain fettuccine**
- 4 **ounces fresh mushrooms, sliced**
- ¼ **cup sliced green onions**
- 2 **tablespoons margarine or butter**
- 2 **tablespoons all-purpose flour**
- ¼ **teaspoon salt**
- ¼ **teaspoon coarsely ground pepper**
- ¼ **teaspoon ground nutmeg**
- 1½ **cups milk**
- ½ **cup grated or finely shredded Parmesan cheese**
- 2 **tablespoons dry sherry**
- 2 **cups cubed cooked chicken (10 ounces)**
- ½ **cup sliced pitted ripe olives**
  Snipped chives (optional)
  Lemon wedges (optional)

Nutrition information per serving: 506 calories, 37 g protein, 42 g carbohydrate, 20 g fat (7 g saturated), 84 mg cholesterol, 639 sodium.

Spinach Fettuccine
With Chicken

Linguine with Chicken And Peanut Sauce

This garlic- and ginger-scented chicken dinner offers an Oriental twist to weeknight fare.

Cook pasta according to package directions. Drain; keep warm.

For sauce, in a medium mixing bowl stir together chicken broth, wine or water, soy sauce, cornstarch, and red pepper. Stir in peanut butter until smooth. Set sauce aside.

In a wok or large skillet heat the cooking oil over medium-high heat. (Add more oil as necessary during cooking.) Add onion, garlic, and gingerroot to hot oil; stir-fry for 2 to 3 minutes or until onion is crisp-tender. Remove onion mixture from skillet.

Add the chicken to the wok. Stir-fry about 3 minutes or till chicken is no longer pink. Push the chicken from the center of the wok. Stir sauce; add to center of the wok. Cook and stir until thickened and bubbly. Cook and stir for 2 minutes more. Return onion mixture to the skillet; stir all the ingredients together.

Arrange pasta on individual plates or a large platter. Spoon the chicken mixture over pasta. Sprinkle with green onions. If desired, garnish with orange slices and grapes.

Makes 4 servings.

8 ounces packaged dried linguine or
   spaghetti
1 14½-ounce can chicken broth
2 tablespoons dry white wine or water
2 tablespoons soy sauce
1 tablespoon cornstarch
⅛ to ¼ teaspoon ground red pepper
½ cup peanut butter
1 tablespoon cooking oil
1 medium onion, halved lengthwise and
   thinly sliced
2 cloves garlic, minced
1 teaspoon grated gingerroot
4 medium skinless, boneless chicken
   breast halves (about 12 ounces),
   cut into 1-inch pieces
2 green onions, sliced (¼ cup)
   Orange slices, cut in half (optional)
   Grapes (optional)

Nutrition information per serving: 579 calories, 35 g protein, 57 g carbohydrate, 23 g fat (5 g saturated), 45 mg cholesterol, 1,038 mg sodium.

Cook pasta according to package directions. Drain; keep warm.

In a small mixing bowl combine 1 tablespoon flour, salt, red pepper, white pepper, and black pepper. Toss flour mixture with chicken to coat. Set aside.

In a large skillet heat the cooking oil over medium-high heat. (Add more oil as necessary during cooking.) Add red sweet or green pepper, onion, chopped jalapeño pepper, and garlic; cook and stir until the vegetables are tender. Remove vegetables with a slotted spoon; set aside.

Add chicken to the skillet. Cook and stir for 4 to 5 minutes or until chicken is no longer pink. Remove chicken from skillet.

Stir 2 tablespoons flour into drippings in skillet. Add chicken broth, milk, and Worcestershire sauce. Cook and stir till thickened and bubbly. Add the Monterey Jack or cheddar cheese, stirring until cheese melts. Stir 1 cup of the hot mixture into the sour cream; return all of the sour cream mixture to skillet. Stir in chicken and vegetables. Cook until heated through. Do not boil.

Arrange pasta on individual plates or a large platter. Spoon the chicken mixture over pasta. If desired, garnish with jalapeño pepper slices.

Makes 4 servings.

Ground red, white, and black peppers multiply the hotness by three in this zippy cream sauce.

- **8 ounces packaged dried spaghetti or fettuccine**
- **1 tablespoon all-purpose flour**
- **½ teaspoon salt**
- **¼ to ½ teaspoon ground red pepper**
- **⅛ to ¼ teaspoon ground white pepper**
- **⅛ to ¼ teaspoon ground black pepper**
- **3 small skinless, boneless chicken breast halves (about 8 ounces total), cut into 1-inch pieces**
- **1 tablespoon cooking oil**
- **1 medium red sweet or green pepper, chopped (1 cup)**
- **1 medium onion, chopped (½ cup)**
- **1 tablespoon chopped, seeded jalapeño pepper**
- **2 cloves garlic, minced**
- **2 tablespoons all-purpose flour**
- **¾ cup chicken broth**
- **½ cup milk**
- **1 teaspoon Worcestershire sauce**
- **1 cup shredded Monterey Jack or cheddar cheese (4 ounces)**
- **¼ cup dairy sour cream**
- **1 jalapeño pepper, thinly sliced (optional)**

Nutrition information per serving: 512 calories, 29 g protein, 56 g carbohydrate, 19 g fat (9 g saturated), 64 mg cholesterol, 660 mg sodium.

Pasta with Chicken and Pepper-Cheese Sauce

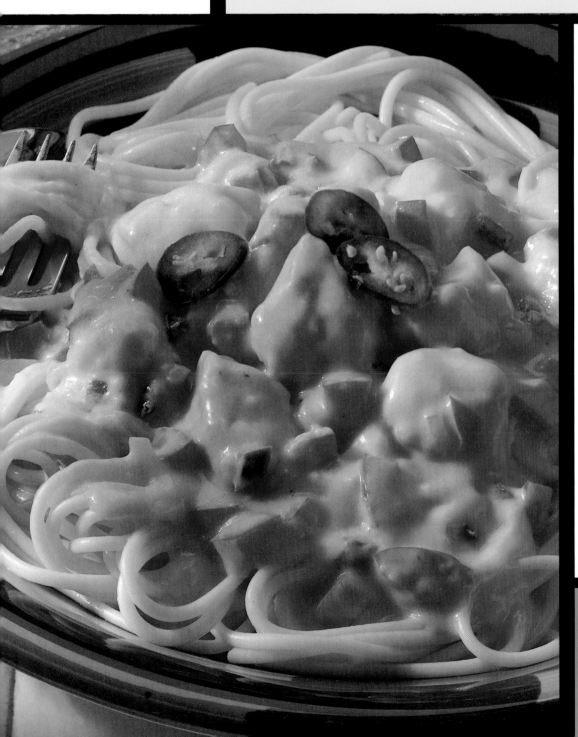

Turkey Lasagna Rolls

For this robust lasagna-style entrée, roll the noodles around a cheesy spinach filling and then top them with a turkey and tomato sauce.

For sauce, in a large skillet cook turkey, onion, and garlic until turkey is no longer pink; drain fat. Stir in mushrooms, water, undrained tomatoes, tomato paste, oregano, and basil. Bring to boiling; reduce heat. Cover and simmer for 25 minutes.

Meanwhile, cook lasagna noodles according to package directions. Drain; rinse with cold water. Drain again.

For filling, in a mixing bowl stir together egg, ricotta cheese, spinach, 1 cup of the mozzarella cheese, and ¾ cup of the Parmesan cheese.

Spread about ½ cup of the filling on each lasagna noodle. Starting from a narrow end, roll up each lasagna noodle. Place lasagna rolls in a 2-quart rectangular baking dish. Pour sauce over lasagna rolls. Cover dish with foil.

Bake in a 375° oven for 25 minutes. Remove foil. Sprinkle with remaining mozzarella cheese. Bake 5 to 10 minutes more or until heated through. Let stand 5 minutes before serving. Sprinkle with remaining Parmesan cheese and, if desired, garnish with parsley sprigs.

Makes 8 servings.

8 ounces ground raw turkey
1 medium onion, chopped (½ cup)
2 cloves garlic, minced
1 cup sliced fresh mushrooms
1 cup water
1 7½-ounce can tomatoes, cut up
1 6-ounce can tomato paste
1½ teaspoons dried oregano, crushed
1 teaspoon dried basil, crushed
8 packaged dried lasagna noodles
1 beaten egg
1 15-ounce carton ricotta cheese
1 10-ounce package frozen chopped spinach, thawed and drained
1½ cups shredded mozzarella cheese (6 ounces)
1 cup grated Parmesan cheese
   Fresh parsley sprigs (optional)

Nutrition information per serving: 345 calories, 26 g protein, 28 g carbohydrate, 15 g fat (8 g saturated), 75 mg cholesterol, 511 mg sodium.

For sauce, in a Dutch oven cook onion, green pepper, carrot, and celery in hot oil until tender. Stir in fresh or undrained canned tomatoes, tomato paste, Italian seasoning, sugar, salt, and garlic powder. Bring to boiling; add Turkey Meatballs. Reduce heat; cover and simmer for 30 minutes. If necessary, uncover and simmer for 10 to 15 minutes more or until sauce is desired consistency, stirring sauce occasionally.

Meanwhile, cook pasta according to package directions; drain.

Arrange pasta on individual plates or a large platter. Spoon the meatballs and sauce over pasta.

Makes 6 servings.

Turkey Meatballs: In a medium mixing bowl combine 1 beaten egg; 2 tablespoons milk; ¼ cup fine dry bread crumbs; ½ teaspoon salt; ½ teaspoon dried Italian seasoning, crushed; and ½ teaspoon pepper. Add 1 pound ground raw turkey; mix well. With wet hands, shape the turkey mixture into twenty-four 1-inch meatballs. Place the meatballs in a greased 13×9×2-inch baking pan. Bake in a 375° oven for 20 minutes or until no pink remains in meat; drain fat.

1 large onion, chopped (1 cup)
1 medium green pepper, coarsely chopped (1 cup)
1 medium carrot, coarsely chopped (½ cup)
1 stalk celery, sliced (½ cup)
1 tablespoon cooking oil
4 large ripe tomatoes, peeled and chopped (4 cups), or two 16-ounce cans tomatoes, cut up
1 6-ounce can (⅔ cup) tomato paste
2 teaspoons dried Italian seasoning, crushed
½ teaspoon sugar
½ teaspoon salt
½ teaspoon garlic powder
Turkey Meatballs
12 ounces packaged dried spaghetti or mostaccioli

Nutrition information per serving: 442 calories, 22 g protein, 65 g carbohydrate, 11 g fat (2 g saturated), 64 mg cholesterol, 686 mg sodium.

Spaghetti with Turkey Meatballs

In a large skillet bring wine or water to boiling. Add frozen fish fillets; cook for 4 minutes. Add shrimp; cook for 2 to 3 minutes more or until fish flakes with a fork and shrimp turn pink. Drain; discarding cooking liquid. Cut fish into bite-size pieces. Coarsely chop shrimp. (If desired, reserve a few whole shrimp for garnish.) Set aside.

Meanwhile, cook lasagna noodles according to package directions. Drain noodles; rinse with cold water. Drain again.

For filling, in a small mixing bowl combine egg, ricotta or cottage cheese, half of the Parmesan cheese, and the basil. Set filling aside.

For sauce, in a medium saucepan cook mushrooms and green onion in margarine or butter until tender. Stir in flour, salt, and pepper. Add milk all at once. Cook and stir until thickened and bubbly. Remove from heat. Stir about 1 cup of the hot mixture into the sour cream; return all the sour cream mixture to the saucepan. Stir fish and shrimp into the sauce.

To assemble, layer half of the cooked noodles in a 2-quart rectangular baking dish. Spread with half of the filling. Top with half of the sauce and half of the mozzarella cheese. Repeat layers. Sprinkle with remaining Parmesan cheese.

Bake in a 375° oven for 30 to 35 minutes or until heated through. Let stand 10 minutes before serving. If desired, garnish with reserved whole shrimp and basil leaves.

Makes 10 servings.

Tender morsels of seafood in a sour cream sauce takes lasagna to new heights.

1½ **cups dry white wine or water**
1 **12-ounce package frozen fish fillets**
1 **8-ounce package frozen, peeled, deveined shrimp**
6 **packaged dried lasagna noodles**
1 **beaten egg**
2 **cups ricotta cheese or cream-style cottage cheese, drained**
½ **cup grated Parmesan cheese**
4 **teaspoons snipped fresh basil or 1 teaspoon dried basil, crushed**
1 **cup sliced fresh mushrooms**
2 **green onions, sliced (¼ cup)**
3 **tablespoons margarine or butter**
3 **tablespoons all-purpose flour**
¼ **teaspoon salt**
¼ **teaspoon ground white pepper**
1⅓ **cups milk**
½ **cup dairy sour cream**
1 **8-ounce package sliced mozzarella cheese**
Fresh basil leaves (optional)

Nutrition information per serving: 336 calories, 28 g protein, 16 g carbohydrate, 17 g fat (9 g saturated), 106 mg cholesterol, 441 mg sodium.

Creamy Seafood Lasagna

Fettuccine with Herbed Shrimp

A white wine and herb sauce dresses the shrimp and pasta in this elegant entrée.

Thaw shrimp, if frozen. Cut shrimp in half lengthwise; set aside.

Cook pasta according to package directions. Drain; keep warm.

Meanwhile, in a large saucepan cook mushrooms, onion, and garlic in hot oil until onion is tender but not brown.

In a small mixing bowl stir together wine, bouillon granules, basil, oregano, cornstarch, and pepper. Add to saucepan. Cook and stir until thickened and bubbly.

Add shrimp to wine mixture. Cover and simmer about 2 minutes or until shrimp turn pink. Stir in tomatoes; heat through.

Spoon the shrimp mixture over pasta. Sprinkle with Parmesan cheese and parsley. Toss to mix.

Makes 4 servings.

12 ounces fresh or frozen, peeled, deveined shrimp

6 ounces packaged dried plain and/or spinach fettuccine

2 cups sliced fresh mushrooms

1 large onion, chopped (1 cup)

2 cloves garlic, minced

1 tablespoon olive oil or cooking oil

¼ cup dry white wine

1 tablespoon instant chicken bouillon granules

1 tablespoon snipped fresh basil or 1 teaspoon dried basil, crushed

1½ teaspoons snipped fresh oregano or ½ teaspoon dried oregano, crushed

1 teaspoon cornstarch

⅛ teaspoon pepper

2 medium tomatoes, peeled, seeded, and chopped

¼ cup grated Parmesan cheese

¼ cup snipped parsley

Nutrition information per serving: 351 calories, 25 g protein, 44 g carbohydrate, 7 g fat (2 g saturated), 136 mg cholesterol, 926 mg sodium.

Linguine with Clams and Dried Tomatoes

Dried tomatoes give a robust flavor to this classic pasta dish. Look for them in specialty shops or the gourmet section of your grocery store.

Cook pasta according to package directions. Drain; keep warm.

Meanwhile, for sauce, drain clams, reserving liquid. In a medium saucepan cook onion, garlic, and crushed red pepper in hot oil. Stir in reserved clam liquid and wine. Bring to boiling. Boil gently about 10 minutes or until sauce is reduced to about 1 cup. Stir in clams, tomatoes, and the 2 tablespoons parsley; heat through.

Arrange the pasta on individual plates or a large platter. Spoon the sauce over the pasta. If desired, garnish with parsley sprigs.

Makes 4 servings.

8 ounces packaged dried linguine, fettuccine, or spaghetti
2 6½-ounce cans chopped or minced clams
1 medium onion, chopped (½ cup)
2 cloves garlic, minced
¼ teaspoon crushed red pepper
2 tablespoons olive oil or cooking oil
½ cup dry white wine
⅓ cup oil-packed dried tomatoes, drained and cut into strips
2 tablespoons snipped parsley
Parsley sprigs (optional)

Nutrition information per serving: 387 calories, 16 g protein, 53 g carbohydrate, 11 g fat (2 g saturated), 57 mg cholesterol, 58 mg sodium.

Linguine with Smoked Salmon In Cream Sauce

If you are using smoked salmon, omit the salt when cooking the pasta. You'll find the smoked salmon adds all the saltiness you need.

Cook pasta according to package directions. Drain; keep warm.

Meanwhile, cut the salmon into thin bite-size strips; set aside.

For sauce, in a large skillet cook the green onion and garlic in margarine or butter until tender. Add salmon and cook for 1 minute. Stir in whipping cream, 1 tablespoon fresh dill or 1 teaspoon dried dillweed, lemon peel, and pepper. Bring to boiling; reduce heat. Cook at a gentle boil about 5 minutes or until the sauce thickens slightly. Remove from heat. Stir in Parmesan cheese.

Arrange the pasta on individual plates or a large platter. Spoon the sauce over the pasta. If desired, garnish with fresh dill sprigs.

Makes 4 servings.

8 ounces packaged dried linguine, fettuccine, or spaghetti
6 ounces thinly sliced, smoked salmon (lox-style) or cooked fresh salmon
2 green onions, thinly sliced (¼ cup)
1 clove garlic, minced
1 tablespoon margarine or butter
1 cup whipping cream
1 tablespoon snipped fresh dill or 1 teaspoon dried dillweed
1 teaspoon finely shredded lemon peel
¼ teaspoon pepper
2 tablespoons grated Parmesan cheese
Fresh dill sprigs (optional)

Nutrition information per serving: 523 calories, 18 g protein, 48 g carbohydrate, 29 g fat (15 g saturated), 94 mg cholesterol, 450 mg sodium.

Spinach and Orzo Pie

Orzo is among the tiniest of pastas. In this dish, it provides a nifty crust for the spinach and ricotta filling.

1½ cups packaged dried orzo (9 ounces)
2 beaten eggs
1 15½-ounce jar chunky spaghetti sauce
⅓ cup grated Parmesan cheese
1 10-ounce package frozen chopped spinach
½ cup ricotta cheese
¼ teaspoon ground nutmeg
½ cup shredded fontina or mozzarella cheese (2 ounces)

Cook pasta according to package directions. Drain pasta; rinse with cold water. Drain again.

In a medium mixing bowl combine eggs, ½ cup of the spaghetti sauce, and Parmesan cheese. Add pasta; toss to coat. Spread pasta mixture over the bottom and up the sides of a greased 9-inch pie plate to form an even shell; set aside.

Cook spinach according to package directions; drain well. In another mixing bowl stir together spinach, ricotta cheese, and nutmeg. Spoon into bottom of the pasta-lined pie plate. Spread remaining spaghetti sauce over the filling. Cover edge of pie with foil.

Bake in a 350° oven for 30 minutes. Sprinkle with fontina or mozzarella cheese. Bake for 3 to 5 minutes more or until cheese melts. Let stand 5 minutes before serving. Cut into wedges.

Makes 6 servings.

Nutrition information per serving: 374 calories, 17 g protein, 49 g carbohydrate, 12 g fat (5 g saturated), 93 mg cholesterol, 617 mg sodium.

Cook pasta according to package directions; drain. Keep warm.

Meanwhile, for sauce, in a small bowl stir together water, cornstarch, and bouillon granules. Set aside.

Pour olive oil into wok or large skillet. Preheat over medium-high heat. Stir-fry garlic in hot oil for 15 seconds. Add asparagus, carrots, and onion; stir-fry for 2 minutes. Add pea pods, almonds or cashews, parsley, basil, and pepper. Stir-fry about 1 minute more or until vegetables are crisp-tender. Remove vegetable mixture from wok.

Stir sauce. Add sauce to wok. Cook and stir till thickened and bubbly. Cook and stir 1 minute more. Return vegetable mixture to wok; toss to coat. Heat through.

To serve, spoon vegetable mixture over hot cooked pasta. Sprinkle with Parmesan cheese.

Makes 4 servings.

- 6 ounces linguine, spaghetti, or fettuccine
- 1 cup water
- 2 teaspoons cornstarch
- 2 teaspoons instant vegetable or chicken bouillon granules
- 1 tablespoon olive oil
- 2 cloves garlic, minced
- 8 ounces fresh asparagus, cut into 1-inch pieces
- 2 medium carrots, very thinly bias-sliced (1 cup)
- 1 medium onion, chopped ($\frac{1}{2}$ cup)
- 1 6-ounce package frozen pea pods, thawed and well drained
- $\frac{2}{3}$ cup sliced almonds or chopped cashews
- $\frac{1}{4}$ cup snipped parsley or 1 tablespoon dried parsley flakes
- 2 tablespoons snipped fresh basil or 1$\frac{1}{2}$ teaspoons dried basil, crushed
- $\frac{1}{4}$ teaspoon pepper
- $\frac{1}{3}$ cup finely shredded Parmesan cheese

Nutrition information per serving: 432 calories, 17 g protein, 52 g carbohydrate, 19 g fat (3 g saturated), 7 mg cholesterol, 642 mg sodium.

Herbed Pasta Primavera

Cook pasta according to package directions. Drain; keep warm.

Meanwhile, for sauce, in a medium saucepan cook carrots, zucchini, and mushrooms in margarine or butter until vegetables are tender. Stir in flour. Add milk all at once. Cook and stir over medium heat until thickened and bubbly. Cook and stir for 1 minute more. Add beer and heat through. Remove pan from heat. Gradually add cheese, stirring just until melted. If desired, season to taste with salt and pepper.

Arrange pasta on individual plates or a large platter. Spoon the sauce over pasta.

Makes 4 servings.

Be sure to use sharp cheddar for the cheesiest flavor.

8 **ounces packaged dried tri-colored corkscrew macaroni or rope macaroni (gemelli)**

2 **medium carrots, bias-sliced (1 cup)**

1 **small zucchini, coarsely chopped (1 cup)**

1 **cup fresh whole mushrooms, quartered**

2 **tablespoons margarine or butter**

2 **tablespoons all-purpose flour**

1 **cup milk**

¼ **cup beer**

¾ **cup shredded sharp cheddar cheese (3 ounces)**

Nutrition information per serving: 426 calories, 16 g protein, 55 g carbohydrate, 15 g fat (6 g saturated), 27 mg cholesterol, 253 mg sodium.

Pasta Twists with Beer-Cheese Sauce

For sauce, in a large saucepan cook onion, celery, and garlic in margarine or butter until tender. Stir in fresh or undrained canned tomatoes, mushrooms, green pepper, sage, sugar, salt, and pepper. Bring to boiling; reduce heat. Simmer, uncovered, for 40 minutes. Add summer squash or zucchini. Cook about 5 minutes more or until sauce is desired consistency and squash is tender.

Meanwhile, cook tortellini according to package directions. Drain. Toss tortellini with sauce.

Makes 4 servings.

1   medium onion, chopped ($\frac{1}{2}$ cup)
1   stalk celery, sliced ($\frac{1}{2}$ cup)
2   cloves garlic, minced
1   tablespoon margarine or butter
2   pounds ripe tomatoes, peeled and
       chopped (3 cups), or one 28-ounce can
       tomatoes, cut up
1   cup sliced fresh mushrooms
$\frac{1}{2}$ cup chopped green pepper
1   tablespoon snipped fresh sage or
       1 teaspoon dried sage, crushed
$\frac{1}{2}$ teaspoon sugar
$\frac{1}{4}$ teaspoon salt
$\frac{1}{8}$ teaspoon pepper
1   small yellow summer squash or zucchini,
       cut into $\frac{1}{2}$-inch pieces
1   8-ounce package dried tortellini or one
       9-ounce package refrigerated tortellini

Nutrition information per serving: 295 calories, 14 g protein, 48 g carbohydrate, 7 g fat (1g saturated), 35 mg cholesterol, 484 mg sodium.

Tortellini with Garden Vegetable Sauce

Sizzling Stir-Fries

Trim fat from beef. Partially freeze beef. Thinly slice across grain into bite-size strips. Set aside.

In a small bowl cover mushrooms with warm water. Let soak for 30 minutes. Rinse and squeeze mushrooms to drain thoroughly. Discard stems. Thinly slice mushrooms. Set aside.

For sauce, in a small bowl stir together bean sauce or paste, sherry, soy sauce, crushed Szechwan pepper or black pepper, cornstarch, and chili oil. Set aside.

Pour cooking oil into a wok or large skillet. (Add more oil as necessary during cooking.) Preheat over medium-high heat. Stir-fry carrots and garlic in hot oil for 2 minutes. Add broccoli; stir-fry for 2 minutes. Add bamboo shoots and mushrooms; stir-fry for 1 to 2 minutes more or until vegetables are crisp-tender. Remove vegetables from wok.

Add beef to the wok. Stir-fry for 2 to 3 minutes or to desired doneness. Push beef from center of wok.

Stir sauce. Add sauce to the center of the wok. Cook and stir till thickened and bubbly. Return cooked vegetables to the wok. Stir all ingredients together to coat with sauce. Cook and stir for 1 minute more or until heated through. Serve immediately with hot cooked rice. Garnish with slivered green onions.

Makes 4 servings.

12 ounces boneless beef sirloin steak

6 dried mushrooms (1 cup), such as shiitake or wood ear mushrooms

¼ cup hot bean sauce or hot bean paste

¼ cup dry sherry

2 tablespoons soy sauce

¾ teaspoon whole Szechwan pepper or whole black pepper, crushed

½ teaspoon cornstarch

½ to 1 teaspoon chili oil

1 tablespoon cooking oil

2 medium carrots, bias-sliced (1 cup)

1 clove garlic, minced

1½ cups broccoli flowerets or one 10-ounce package frozen cut broccoli, thawed

1 8-ounce can bamboo shoots, drained

2 cups hot cooked rice

2 green onions, cut into slivers (¼ cup)

Nutrition information per serving: 387 calories, 25 g protein, 53 g carbohydrate, 9 g fat (2 g saturated fat), 49 mg cholesterol, 1,615 mg sodium.

Szechwan Beef Stir-Fry

Thai Beef Larnar

In Thai cuisine, fish sauce is a common ingredient used to salt foods. In this recipe it seasons the nam prik—Thailand's version of bottled hot pepper sauce.

2 to 4 dried red chili peppers*

¼ cup water

2 tablespoons lemon juice

2 tablespoons soy sauce

1 tablespoon cooking oil

1 to 1½ teaspoons fish sauce or nuoc cham

2 to 4 cloves garlic, quartered

1 pound beef top round steak

1 tablespoon cooking oil

4 cups broccoli flowerets

2 cups hot cooked rice

For nam prik, cut open dried chili peppers. Discard stems and seeds; cut up peppers. Place peppers in a bowl and cover with boiling water. Let stand for 45 minutes to 1 hour. Drain. In a blender container combine peppers, water, lemon juice, soy sauce, cooking oil, fish sauce or nuoc cham, and garlic. Cover and blend until mixture is nearly smooth. Set aside. Trim fat from beef. Partially freeze beef. Thinly slice across grain into bite-size strips. Set aside.

Pour cooking oil into a wok or large skillet. (Add more oil as necessary during cooking.) Preheat over medium-high heat. Stir-fry broccoli in hot oil for 3 to 4 minutes or until crisp-tender. Remove broccoli from the wok.

Add half of the beef to the wok. Stir-fry for 2 to 3 minutes or to desired doneness. Remove beef from the wok. Repeat with remaining beef. Return all beef to the wok.

Stir nam prik; add to the center of the wok. Return the broccoli to the wok. Stir all ingredients together to coat with nam prik. Bring to boiling. Cover and cook 1 minute more or until heated through. Serve immediately with hot cooked rice.

Makes 4 servings.

*Note: You can substitute ½ to 1 teaspoon crushed red pepper for the dried red chili peppers. Skip the soaking step and continue as directed.

Nutrition information per serving: 363 calories, 33 g protein, 30 g carbohydrate, 13 g fat (3 g saturated fat), 73 mg cholesterol, 662 mg sodium.

Pork and Pear Stir-Fry

Plum preserves, pears, and gingerroot give this delicious pork entrée its special sweetness.

Trim fat from pork. Partially freeze pork. Thinly slice across grain into bite-size strips. Set aside.

For sauce, in a small bowl stir together preserves, soy sauce, lemon juice, horseradish, cornstarch, and crushed red pepper. Set aside.

Pour cooking oil into a wok or large skillet. (Add more oil as necessary during cooking.) Preheat over medium-high heat. Stir-fry gingerroot in hot oil for 15 seconds. Add sweet pepper and pear; stir-fry for 1½ minutes. Remove pear mixture from the wok.

Add half of the pork to the hot wok. Stir-fry for 2 to 3 minutes or until no pink remains. Remove pork from the wok. Repeat with remaining pork. Return all of the pork to the wok. Push pork from the center of the wok.

Stir sauce. Add sauce to the center of the wok. Cook and stir until slightly thickened and bubbly.

Return pear mixture to the wok. Add water chestnuts. Stir all ingredients together to coat with sauce. Cook and stir for 2 minutes. Top with pea pods. Cover and cook for 1 to 2 minutes more or until heated through. Serve immediately with hot cooked rice.

Makes 4 servings.

1 pound pork tenderloin
½ cup plum preserves
3 tablespoons soy sauce
2 tablespoons lemon juice
1 tablespoon prepared horseradish
2 teaspoons cornstarch
½ teaspoon crushed red pepper
1 tablespoon cooking oil
2 teaspoons grated gingerroot
1 medium yellow or green sweet pepper, cut into julienne strips (1 cup)
1 medium pear, cored and sliced (1 cup)
⅓ cup sliced water chestnuts
1½ cups fresh pea pods, strings removed, or 4 ounces frozen pea pods, thawed
2 cups hot cooked rice

Nutrition information per serving: 473 calories, 30 g protein, 70 g carbohydrate, 8 g fat (2 g saturated fat), 81 mg cholesterol, 884 mg sodium.

Stir-Fried Pork
And Jicama

Though jicama (HE-kuh-muh) is a Mexican vegetable, it adds some crispness to this Chinese-inspired dish.

Trim fat from pork. Partially freeze pork. Thinly slice across grain into bite-size strips. Set aside.

For sauce, in a small bowl stir together water, sherry, soy sauce, and cornstarch. Set aside.

Pour cooking oil into a wok or large skillet. (Add more oil as necessary during cooking.) Preheat over medium-high heat. Stir-fry gingerroot and garlic in hot oil for 15 seconds. Add jicama, sweet pepper strips, and green onion; stir-fry 1 to 2 minutes or until crisp-tender. Remove vegetables from the wok.

Add half of the pork to the hot wok. Stir-fry for 2 to 3 minutes or until no pink remains. Remove pork from the wok. Repeat with remaining pork. Return all of the pork to wok. Push pork from center of wok.

Stir sauce. Add sauce to the center of the wok. Cook and stir till thickened and bubbly. Add cooked vegetables. Stir all ingredients together to coat with sauce. Add spinach or cabbage. Cook and stir 1 to 2 minutes more or until heated through. Serve immediately with hot cooked rice.

Makes 4 servings.

1   **pound lean boneless pork**
½   **cup cold water**
¼   **cup dry sherry**
¼   **cup soy sauce**
4   **teaspoons cornstarch**
1   **tablespoon cooking oil**
1   **teaspoon grated gingerroot**
1   **clove garlic, minced**
½   **of a medium jicama, peeled and cut into julienne strips (1 cup)**
1   **medium red and/or green sweet pepper, cut into thin strips**
1   **green onion, sliced (2 tablespoons)**
2   **cups shredded spinach or Chinese cabbage**
2   **cups hot cooked rice**

Nutrition information per serving: 341 calories, 21 g protein, 35 g carbohydrate, 11 g fat (3 g saturated fat), 51 mg cholesterol, 1,080 mg sodium.

Trim fat from pork. Partially freeze pork. Thinly slice across grain into bite-size strips. In a medium bowl stir together pork, 2 tablespoons soy sauce, sesame oil, gingerroot, and garlic. Cover and refrigerate for 1 to 2 hours.

For sauce, in a small bowl stir together hoisin sauce, water, 2 tablespoons soy sauce, cornstarch, sugar, and crushed red pepper. Set sauce aside.

Pour cooking oil into a wok or large skillet. (Add more oil as necessary during cooking.) Preheat over medium-high heat. Stir-fry onions and celery in hot oil for 1 minute. Add broccoli; stir-fry for 3 to 4 minutes or until the vegetables are crisp-tender. Remove vegetables from the wok.

Add pork mixture to the hot wok. Stir-fry for 2 to 3 minutes or until no pink remains. Push pork from the center of the wok.

Stir sauce. Add sauce to the center of the wok. Cook and stir until sauce is thickened and bubbly. Return cooked vegetables to the wok. Stir all ingredients together to coat with sauce. Cover and cook for 1 minute more or until heated through. Serve immediately with hot cooked rice. Sprinkle with cashews.

Makes 4 servings.

12	ounces lean boneless pork
2	tablespoons soy sauce
2	teaspoons toasted sesame oil
2	teaspoons grated gingerroot
2	cloves garlic, minced
½	cup hoisin sauce
½	cup water
2	tablespoons soy sauce
1	tablespoon cornstarch
1	teaspoon sugar
⅛	teaspoon crushed red pepper
1	tablespoon cooking oil
2	medium onions, cut into thin wedges
2	stalks celery, thinly bias-sliced (1 cup)
3	cups broccoli flowerets
2	cups hot cooked rice
½	cup dry roasted cashews

Nutrition information per serving: 480 calories, 21 g protein, 42 g carbohydrate, 26 g fat (5 g saturated fat), 38 mg cholesterol, 1,554 mg sodium.

Cashew Pork and Broccoli

Greek Lamb Stir-Fry

Oregano and rosemary join with fresh lemon juice, olive oil, and feta cheese to lend this delicious lamb dish some of the characteristic flavors of Greece.

Trim fat from lamb. Partially freeze lamb. Thinly slice across grain into bite-size strips. Set aside.

For sauce, in a small bowl combine 1 tablespoon oil, lemon juice or vinegar, rosemary, oregano, and pepper. Set aside.

Pour 1 tablespoon cooking oil into a wok or large skillet. (Add more oil as necessary during cooking.) Preheat over medium-high heat. Stir-fry garlic in hot oil for 15 seconds. Add carrot and onion; stir-fry 3 to 4 minutes or until crisp-tender. Remove vegetables from wok.

Add lamb to the hot wok. Stir-fry for 2 to 3 minutes or to desired doneness. Return cooked carrot and onion to the wok. Add sauce, spinach, and tomato wedges. Stir all ingredients together to coat with sauce. Remove from heat. Serve immediately over hot cooked rice, if desired. Top with crumbled feta cheese.

Makes 3 servings.

8 ounces lean boneless lamb

1 tablespoon cooking oil

1 tablespoon lemon juice or balsamic vinegar

½ teaspoon dried rosemary, crushed

½ teaspoon dried oregano, crushed

¼ teaspoon pepper

1 tablespoon cooking oil

1 clove garlic, minced

1 medium carrot, thinly bias-sliced (½ cup)

1 small red onion, thinly sliced (⅓ cup)

4 cups torn fresh spinach (about 5 ounces)

2 small tomatoes, cut into thin wedges

2 cups hot cooked rice (optional)

¼ cup crumbled feta cheese (1 ounce)

Nutrition information per serving: 243 calories, 16 g protein, 11 g carbohydrate, 16 g fat (4 g saturated fat), 45 mg cholesterol, 208 mg sodium.

In a saucepan cook rice sticks in boiling water for 3 minutes. (Or, cook vermicelli according to package directions.) Drain. Set aside; keep warm.

Meanwhile, rinse chicken; pat dry with paper towels. Cut chicken thighs or breasts into thin, bite-sized strips; set aside.

For sauce, combine chicken broth, soy sauce, basil, cornstarch, chili oil or crushed red pepper, and turmeric; set aside.

Add cooking oil to wok or 12-inch skillet. Preheat over medium-high heat (add more oil if necessary during cooking). Stir-fry carrot strips in hot oil for 1 minute. Add broccoli flowerets; stir-fry for 2 minutes more. Add red or green sweet pepper strips; stir-fry for 1½ to 3 minutes more or until crisp-tender. Remove vegetables from wok. Add chicken to wok; stir-fry for 2 to 3 minutes or until no longer pink. Push chicken from center of wok.

Stir sauce; add to center of wok. Cook and stir until thickened and bubbly. Return vegetables to wok. Stir to coat. Cook and stir 2 minutes more or until heated through. Serve immediately over hot rice sticks or vermicelli. Top with cashews or peanuts.

Makes 4 servings.

3 ounces rice sticks (also called rice noodles) or thin vermicelli, broken

12 ounces skinless, boneless chicken thighs or breasts

½ cup chicken broth

2 tablespoons soy sauce

2 tablespoons snipped fresh basil or 2 teaspoons dried basil, crushed

2 teaspoons cornstarch

1 teaspoon chili oil or ½ teaspoon crushed red pepper

½ teaspoon ground turmeric

1 tablespoon cooking oil

2 medium carrots, cut into julienne strips

2 cups broccoli flowerets

1 red or green sweet pepper, cut into 1-inch strips (½ cup)

¼ cup cashew halves or peanuts

Nutrition information per serving: 309 calories, 17 g protein, 32 g carbohydrate, 13 g fat (3 g saturated), 41 mg cholesterol, 748 mg sodium.

Pacific Rim Stir-Fry

Rinse chicken and pat dry. Cut into 1-inch pieces. Set aside.

For sauce, in a small bowl stir together hoisin sauce, soy sauce, water, and sugar. Set aside.

In a medium saucepan precook long beans, covered, in small amount of boiling water for 3 to 5 minutes (cook whole green beans about 10 minutes) or until crisp-tender. Drain. Set aside.

Pour cooking oil into a wok or large skillet. (Add more oil as necessary during cooking.) Preheat over medium-high heat. Stir-fry garlic in hot oil for 15 seconds. Add onion; stir-fry about 3 minutes or until crisp-tender. Remove onion mixture from wok.

Add walnuts to wok; stir-fry for 2 to 3 minutes or until golden. Remove walnuts from the wok.

Add chicken to the hot wok; stir-fry for 3 to 4 minutes or until no pink remains. Return onion mixture and walnuts to the wok. Add beans.

Stir sauce. Add sauce to the wok. Stir all ingredients together to coat with sauce. Cook and stir for 1 to 2 minutes more or until heated through. Serve immediately over hot cooked rice.

Makes 4 servings.

Yard-long beans, more commonly called Chinese long beans, can grow to a length of 18 inches, but they cook in much less time than regular green beans.

12 ounces skinless, boneless chicken breast halves

2 tablespoons hoisin sauce

1 tablespoon soy sauce

1 tablespoon water

½ teaspoon sugar

8 ounces fresh Chinese long beans, cut into 4-inch lengths, or 8 ounces fresh whole green beans

1 tablespoon cooking oil

3 cloves garlic, minced

1 medium onion, cut into thin wedges

½ cup coarsely broken walnuts

2 cups hot cooked rice

Nutrition information per serving: 363 calories, 23 g protein, 34 g carbohydrate, 16 g fat (2 g saturated fat), 45 mg cholesterol, 817 mg sodium.

Chicken with Long Beans And Walnuts

Rinse chicken and pat dry. Cut into 1-inch pieces. In a medium bowl combine coriander, cumin, turmeric, nutmeg, cinnamon, ground red pepper, and cloves. Add chicken; stir to coat. Set aside.

For sauce, in a small bowl stir together water, vinegar, sugar, cornstarch, and salt. Set aside.

Pour cooking oil into a wok or large skillet. (Add more oil as necessary during cooking.) Preheat over medium-high heat. Stir-fry gingerroot and garlic in hot oil for 15 seconds. Add onions, sweet pepper, and lemon grass or lemon peel; stir-fry for 2 to 3 minutes or until vegetables are crisp-tender. Remove vegetables from the wok. Discard lemon grass, if used.

Add chicken mixture to the hot wok. Stir-fry chicken for 3 to 4 minutes or until no pink remains, scraping the bottom of the wok constantly to prevent spices from sticking. Push chicken from the center of the wok.

Stir sauce. Add sauce to the center of the wok. Cook and stir until thickened and bubbly. Return cooked vegetables to the wok. Stir all ingredients together to coat with sauce. Cook and stir for 1 to 2 minutes more or until heated through. Serve immediately with hot cooked couscous or rice. Sprinkle with peanuts.

Makes 4 servings.

This Malaysian dish shows a blend of both Indian and Asian influences.

- 12 **ounces skinless, boneless chicken thighs**
- 2 **teaspoons ground coriander**
- 1 1/2 **teaspoons ground cumin**
- 1 **teaspoon ground turmeric**
- 1 **teaspoon ground nutmeg**
- 3/4 **teaspoon ground cinnamon**
- 1/4 **teaspoon ground red pepper**
- 1/4 **teaspoon ground cloves**
- 2/3 **cup water**
- 1/4 **cup cider vinegar**
- 3 **tablespoons sugar**
- 1 **tablespoon cornstarch**
- 1/2 **teaspoon salt**
- 1 **tablespoon cooking oil**
- 1 **tablespoon grated gingerroot**
- 4 **cloves garlic, minced**
- 2 **medium onions, cut into thin wedges**
- 1 **medium red or green sweet pepper, cut into strips (1 cup)**
- 1/2 **stalk lemon grass, cut into 2-inch pieces, or 1/2 teaspoon finely shredded lemon peel**
- 2 **cups hot cooked couscous or rice**
- 3 **tablespoons coarsely chopped roasted peanuts**

Nutrition information per serving: 350 calories, 19 g protein, 44 g carbohydrate, 12 g fat (2 g saturated fat), 41 mg cholesterol, 456 mg sodium.

Fragrant Spiced Chicken

Sweet and Sour Chicken

Rinse chicken; pat dry with paper towels. Cut chicken into 1-inch pieces. In a medium bowl combine egg, biscuit mix, and water. Dip chicken pieces into batter to coat.

Heat 1½ cups cooking oil in wok or small deep-fat fryer over medium heat (375°). Fry chicken pieces in hot oil, a few at a time, until golden brown (about 2 minutes). Remove chicken pieces as they brown and drain on paper towels. Discard cooking oil. Keep chicken warm in a 300° oven.

For sauce, drain pineapple, reserving juice. Add enough water to juice to make 1¾ cups. In a bowl combine sugar, soy sauce, vinegar, cornstarch, and paprika. Add pineapple juice mixture; set aside.

Add 1 tablespoon cooking oil to wok or 12-inch skillet. Preheat over medium-high heat. Stir-fry green sweet pepper and green onions in hot oil for 2 to 3 minutes or until crisp-tender. Remove vegetables from wok. Stir sauce; add to center of wok. Cook and stir until slightly thickened and bubbly. Add cooked vegetables, pineapple chunks, and tomatoes to wok. Cook and stir about 2 minutes more or until heated through. Add chicken; stir to coat. Serve immediately over cooked rice.

Makes 6 servings.

Nutrition information per serving: 482 calories, 20 g protein, 60 g carbohydrate, 19 g fat (3 g saturated), 75 mg cholesterol, 843 mg sodium.

1 pound skinless, boneless chicken breasts or thighs
1 beaten egg
1 cup packaged biscuit mix
⅓ cup water
1½ cups cooking oil
1 20-ounce can pineapple chunks (juice pack)
⅓ cup sugar
¼ cup soy sauce
¼ cup cider vinegar
2 tablespoons cornstarch
2 teaspoons paprika
1 tablespoon cooking oil
1 large green sweet pepper, cut lengthwise into strips
4 green onions, cut into 2-inch lengths
2 cups cherry tomatoes, halved
Hot cooked rice

Chicken-Mushroom Lo Mein

Enjoy lo mein at home without calling for take-out—it's easy and tastes terrific.

Rinse chicken; pat dry with paper towels. Cut chicken into thin, bite-sized strips. In a small bowl stir together soy sauce, dry sherry, and cornstarch. Add chicken; stir to coat. Cover and chill for 30 minutes.

Meanwhile, cook linguine according to package directions, omitting oil and salt. Drain well.

Add cooking oil and sesame oil to a wok or 12-inch skillet. Preheat over medium-high heat (add more oil if necessary during cooking). Add mushrooms, red or green sweet peppers, and green onions to wok; stir-fry for 2 minutes. Add pea pods and stir-fry about 1 minute more or until vegetables are crisp-tender. Remove vegetables from wok.

Drain chicken, reserving liquid. Stir-fry chicken for 2 to 3 minutes or until no longer pink. Combine water, bouillon granules, and reserved marinade; add to wok. Cook and stir until thickened and bubbly. Add drained linguine and cooked vegetables. Stir to coat. Cook and stir about 1 minute more or until heated through.

Makes 4 servings.

12 ounces skinless, boneless chicken breasts or thighs
2 tablespoons soy sauce
2 tablespoons dry sherry
2 teaspoons cornstarch
8 ounces linguine
1 tablespoon cooking oil
1 tablespoon toasted sesame oil
8 ounces fresh mushrooms, sliced (3 cups)
1 medium red or green sweet pepper, cut into 2-inch strips (1 cup)
4 green onions, cut into 2-inch pieces
6 ounces fresh pea pods, strings removed (1½ cups)
½ cup water
¼ teaspoon instant chicken bouillon granules

Nutrition information per serving: 434 calories, 28 g protein, 54 g carbohydrate, 11 g fat (2 g saturated), 45 mg cholesterol, 616 mg sodium.

Creamy Turkey Dijon

Mustard, onion, and garlic add zest to this upscale version of an old favorite—turkey à la king. Serve it over noodles or fettuccine for a classy, enjoyable pasta dish.

Rinse turkey and pat dry. Cut into thin bite-size strips. Set aside.

For sauce, in a small bowl stir together flour, mustard, wine, salt, and pepper until smooth. Slowly stir in half-and-half or light cream until well mixed. Set aside.

Pour cooking oil into a wok or large skillet. (Add more oil as necessary during cooking.) Preheat over medium-high heat. Stir-fry garlic in hot oil for 15 seconds. Add sweet pepper and onion; stir-fry for 2 minutes. Add sliced mushrooms; stir-fry for 2 minutes more or until crisp-tender. Remove vegetables from the wok.

Add turkey to the hot wok. Stir-fry for 2 to 3 minutes or until no pink remains. Push turkey from the center of the wok.

Stir sauce. Add sauce to the center of the wok. Cook and stir until thickened and bubbly. Return cooked vegetables to the wok. Add thawed peas. Stir all ingredients together to coat with sauce. Cook and stir for 1 to 2 minutes more or until heated through. Serve immediately over hot cooked noodles or fettuccine. Garnish with whole mushrooms and fresh basil, if desired.

Makes 4 servings.

Nutrition information per serving: 463 calories, 28 g protein, 52 g carbohydrate, 15 g fat (6 g saturated fat), 108 mg cholesterol, 553 mg sodium.

12 **ounces turkey breast tenderloin steaks**
 2 **tablespoons all-purpose flour**
 2 **tablespoons Dijon-style mustard**
 2 **tablespoons dry white wine**
 ½ **teaspoon salt**
 ⅛ **teaspoon pepper**
 1 **cup half-and-half or light cream**
 1 **tablespoon cooking oil**
 1 **clove garlic, minced**
 1 **medium red or green sweet pepper, cut into julienne strips (1 cup)**
 1 **medium onion, chopped (½ cup)**
1½ **cups sliced fresh mushrooms**
 ¾ **cup frozen peas, thawed**
 2 **cups hot cooked noodles or fettuccine**
    Fresh whole mushrooms (optional)
    Fresh basil sprigs (optional)

Tuna with
Vegetables
And Linguine

Fresh tuna—and other firm-fleshed fish—is well suited to stir-frying because it holds its shape well while being quickly cooked and stirred.

12 ounces fresh or frozen tuna steaks or fillets (1 inch thick)
½ cup dry white wine
1 teaspoon dried thyme, crushed
½ teaspoon salt
⅛ to ¼ teaspoon crushed red pepper
1 tablespoon cooking oil
2 cloves garlic, minced
2 cups broccoli flowerets
1 large red or green sweet pepper, cut into julienne strips (1½ cups)
8 ounces linguine, cooked and drained
¾ cup finely shredded Romano or Parmesan cheese

Thaw fish, if frozen. Cut into 1-inch cubes. Discard any skin and bones. Set aside.

For sauce, in a small bowl stir together wine, thyme, salt, and crushed red pepper. Set aside.

Pour cooking oil into a wok or large skillet. (Add more oil as necessary during cooking.) Preheat over medium-high heat. Stir-fry garlic in hot oil for 15 seconds. Add broccoli; stir-fry for 2 minutes. Add sweet pepper; stir-fry for 1 to 2 minutes more or until vegetables are crisp-tender. Remove vegetables from the wok.

Add tuna to the hot wok. Stir-fry for 3 to 6 minutes or until tuna flakes easily, being careful not to break up pieces. Return cooked vegetables to the wok.

Stir sauce. Add sauce to the wok. Add cooked linguine. Gently toss all ingredients together to coat with sauce. Cook and stir 1 to 2 minutes more or until heated through. Remove from heat. Serve immediately. Sprinkle each serving with Romano or Parmesan cheese.

Makes 4 servings.

Nutrition information per serving: 512 calories, 38 g protein, 51 g carbohydrate, 15 g fat (5 g saturated fat), 57 mg cholesterol, 574 mg sodium.

Thaw shrimp, if frozen. Set aside.

For sauce, in a small bowl stir together coconut milk, fish sauce, and white pepper. Set aside.

Pour cooking oil into a wok or 12-inch skillet. (Add more oil as necessary during cooking.) Preheat over medium-high heat. Stir-fry garlic in hot oil for 15 seconds. Add asparagus; stir-fry for 2 minutes. Add mushrooms; stir-fry for 1 to 2 minutes more or until vegetables are crisp-tender. Remove vegetables from the wok.

Add half of the shrimp to the hot wok. Stir-fry for 2 to 3 minutes or until shrimp turn pink. Remove shrimp from the wok. Repeat with remaining shrimp. Return all shrimp to the wok. Push shrimp from center of wok.

Stir sauce. Add sauce to the center of the wok. Cook and stir until bubbly. Return cooked vegetables to the wok. Stir all ingredients together to coat with sauce. Cook and stir 1 minute more or until heated through. Toss together rice and snipped cilantro or parsley. Arrange rice mixture on a serving platter or 4 individual plates. Spoon shrimp mixture over rice mixture. Serve immediately. Garnish with cilantro or parsley sprigs, if desired.

Makes 4 servings.

1 **pound fresh or frozen peeled and deveined medium shrimp**
¾ **cup canned unsweetened coconut milk**
2 **tablespoons fish sauce**
½ **teaspoon white pepper**
1 **tablespoon cooking oil**
4 **cloves garlic, minced**
12 **ounces fresh asparagus, woody ends trimmed, and bias-cut into 1-inch pieces (2¼ cups)**
8 **ounces fresh mushrooms, quartered (3 cups)**
2 **cups hot cooked rice**
2 **tablespoons snipped cilantro or parsley Cilantro or parsley sprigs (optional)**

Nutrition information per serving: 375 calories, 25 g protein, 30 g carbohydrate, 17 g fat (10 g saturated fat), 177 mg cholesterol, 487 mg sodium.

Coconut Shrimp with Garlic

Almond Shrimp in Plum Sauce

Plums, cucumber, and onion make this sweet-and-sour dish especially tasty. Toasted almonds lend additional flavor and a bit of crunch!

Thaw shrimp, if frozen. Set aside.

For sauce, in a small bowl stir together orange juice, water, sugar, hoisin sauce, vinegar, cornstarch, and pepper. Set aside.

Preheat a wok or large skillet over medium-high heat. Add almonds; stir-fry for 2 to 3 minutes or until golden. Remove almonds from the wok. Let wok cool.

Pour cooking oil into the cooled wok. (Add more oil as necessary during cooking.) Preheat over medium-high heat. Stir-fry gingerroot in hot oil for 15 seconds. Add onion; stir-fry for 3 to 4 minutes or until crisp-tender. Add plums and cucumber; stir-fry for 2 minutes more. Remove plum mixture from the wok.

Add shrimp to the hot wok. Stir-fry for 2 to 3 minutes or till shrimp turn pink. Push shrimp from the center of the wok.

Stir sauce. Add sauce to the center of the wok. Cook and stir until thickened and bubbly. Return plum mixture to the wok. Stir all ingredients together to coat with sauce. Cook and stir for 1 to 2 minutes more or until heated through. Serve immediately with hot cooked rice. Sprinkle with toasted almonds.

Makes 4 servings.

12 ounces fresh or frozen peeled and
    deveined medium shrimp
¼ cup orange juice
¼ cup water
3 tablespoons sugar
3 tablespoons hoisin sauce
2 tablespoons vinegar
4 teaspoons cornstarch
¼ teaspoon pepper
3 tablespoons slivered almonds
1 tablespoon cooking oil
1½ teaspoons grated gingerroot
1 medium onion, chopped (½ cup)
4 medium red plums, pitted and thinly
    sliced (2 cups)
1 medium cucumber, seeded and
    chopped (1¼ cup)
2 cups hot cooked rice

Nutrition information per serving: 345 calories, 19 g protein, 51 g carbohydrate, 8 g fat (1 g saturated fat), 131 mg cholesterol, 926 mg sodium.

Vegetarian Fried Rice

Transform fried rice from a side dish into a sumptuous meal by adding extra eggs and lots of vegetables.

In a small bowl combine eggs and 1 tablespoon soy sauce. Set aside.

Pour 1 tablespoon cooking oil into a wok or large skillet. Preheat over medium heat. Stir-fry chopped onion and garlic in hot oil about 2 minutes or until crisp-tender. Add egg mixture and stir gently to scramble. When set, remove egg mixture from the wok. Cut up any large pieces of egg mixture. Let wok cool.

Pour 1 tablespoon cooking oil into the cooled wok or skillet. (Add more oil as necessary during cooking.) Preheat over medium-high heat. Stir-fry celery in hot oil for 1 minute. Add mushrooms and sweet pepper; stir-fry for 1 to 2 minutes more or until vegetables are crisp-tender.

Add cooked rice, bamboo shoots, carrots, and peas. Sprinkle with 3 tablespoons soy sauce. Cook and stir for 4 to 6 minutes or until heated through. Add cooked egg mixture and green onions; cook and stir about 1 minute more or until heated through. Serve immediately. Garnish with carrot slices, if desired.

Makes 4 to 5 servings.

5 eggs, beaten
1 tablespoon soy sauce
1 tablespoon cooking oil
1 small onion, chopped ($\frac{1}{3}$ cup)
1 clove garlic, minced
1 tablespoon cooking oil
2 stalks celery, thinly bias-sliced (1 cup)
4 ounces fresh mushrooms, sliced
    ($1\frac{1}{2}$ cups)
1 medium green sweet pepper,
    chopped ($\frac{3}{4}$ cup)
4 cups cold cooked rice
1 8-ounce can bamboo shoots, drained
2 medium carrots, shredded (1 cup)
$\frac{3}{4}$ cup frozen peas, thawed
3 tablespoons soy sauce
3 green onions, sliced ($\frac{1}{3}$ cup)
    Crinkle-cut carrot slices (optional)

Nutrition information per serving: 438 calories, 17 g protein, 61 g carbohydrate, 14 g fat (3 g saturated fat), 266 mg cholesterol, 1,177 mg sodium.

Mu Shu Vegetable Roll-Ups

Instead of wrapping up our Mu Shu vegetables in the traditional Peking pancakes, we went Mexican and used ready-made flour tortillas.

2 tablespoons water
2 tablespoons soy sauce
½ teaspoon sugar
½ teaspoon cornstarch
8 or 10 8-inch flour tortillas
1 tablespoon cooking oil
1 teaspoon grated gingerroot
2 cloves garlic, minced
2 medium carrots, cut into julienne strips (1 cup)
½ of a small head of cabbage, shredded (3 cups)
1 medium zucchini, cut into julienne strips (1¼ cups)
8 ounces fresh bean sprouts (2 cups)
4 ounces fresh mushrooms, sliced (1½ cups)
½ of a medium jicama, peeled and cut into julienne strips (1 cup)
8 ounces firm tofu (bean curd), well drained and cut into ¾-inch cubes
8 green onions, sliced (1 cup)
¼ cup hoisin sauce
  Cherry tomato flowers (optional)
  Green onion brushes (optional)

For sauce, in a small bowl stir together water, soy sauce, sugar, and cornstarch. Set aside.

Stack tortillas; wrap in foil. Heat in a 350° oven for 10 minutes or till warm. Or, place tortillas, half at a time, between layers of microwave-safe paper towels. Micro-cook on 100% power (high) for 1½ to 2 minutes or until warm.

Meanwhile, pour oil into a wok or large skillet. (Add more oil as necessary during cooking.) Preheat over medium-high heat. Stir-fry gingerroot and garlic in hot oil for 15 seconds. Add carrots; stir-fry for 1 minute. Add cabbage and zucchini; stir-fry for 1 minute. Add bean sprouts, mushrooms, and jicama; stir-fry for 1 to 2 minutes more or until vegetables are crisp-tender. Push vegetables from the center of the wok.

Stir sauce. Add sauce to the center of the wok. Cook and stir until thickened and bubbly. Add tofu and green onions. Gently stir all ingredients together to coat with sauce. Cover and cook for 2 minutes more or until heated through.

Spread warm tortillas with hoisin sauce. Spoon vegetable mixture onto each tortilla. Fold over one side of the tortilla to cover some of the filling. Then, fold the two adjacent sides of the tortilla over the filling. Secure with toothpicks, if necessary. Serve immediately. Garnish with tomato flowers and green onion brushes, if desired.

Makes 4 or 5 servings.

Nutrition information per serving: 399 calories, 20 g protein, 57 g carbohydrate, 12 g fat (2 g saturated), 0 mg cholesterol, 1,811 mg sodium.

For sauce, in a small bowl stir together water, dry sherry or wine, soy sauce, cornstarch, and sugar. Set aside.

Pour the cooking oil into a wok or large skillet. (Add more oil as necessary during cooking.)Preheat the wok or large skillet over medium-high heat. Stir-fry the gingerroot in hot oil for 15 seconds. Add the fresh asparagus (if using) and squash; stir-fry for 3 minutes. Add the thawed asparagus (if using) and green onions; stir-fry about 1½ minutes more or until the asparagus is crisp-tender. Remove vegetables from wok.

Add tofu to the hot wok or skillet. Carefully stir-fry for 2 to 3 minutes or until lightly browned. Remove from wok. Stir the sauce. Add sauce to hot wok. Cook and stir until thickened and bubbly. Return cooked vegetables and tofu to the wok. Stir all ingredients together to coat with sauce. Cover and cook about 1 minute more or until heated through. Stir in pine nuts or almonds. Serve over rice.

Makes 4 servings.

1 cup water
¼ cup dry sherry or dry white wine
2 tablespoons soy sauce
4 teaspoons cornstarch
½ teaspoon sugar
1 tablespoon cooking oil
2 teaspoons grated gingerroot
1 pound fresh asparagus, cut into 1-inch pieces (3 cups), or one 10-ounce package frozen cut asparagus, thawed and well drained
1 small yellow summer squash, halved lengthwise and sliced (1¼ cups)
2 green onions, sliced (¼ cup)
1 10½-ounce package extra firm tofu (fresh bean curd), cut into ½-inch cubes
½ cup pine nuts or chopped almonds, toasted
2 cups hot cooked brown rice

Nutrition information per serving: 412 calories, 22 g protein, 38 g carbohydrate, 21 g fat (3 g saturated), 0 mg cholesterol, 541 mg sodium.

Gingered Vegetable-Tofu Stir-Fry

Pizzas, Sandwiches, And More

Prepare Cornmeal Pizza Dough. Grease two 11- to 13-inch pizza pans or baking sheets. On a lightly floured surface, roll each half of dough into a circle 1 inch larger than pizza pan. Transfer dough to pans. Build up edges slightly. Flute edges, if desired. Prick generously with a fork. Do not let rise. Bake in a 425° oven for 10 to 12 minutes or until lightly browned.

Meanwhile, in a large skillet cook ground beef and onion until meat is brown and onion is tender. Drain fat. Stir in tomato sauce, olives, and taco seasoning mix; heat through.

Spread ground beef mixture over hot crusts. Sprinkle with cheese. Bake about 12 minutes or until cheese melts. Top with lettuce, tomatoes, and avocados. Spoon sour cream into center of each pizza. Sprinkle sour cream with chili powder, if desired.

Makes 6 servings.

Cornmeal Pizza Dough: Prepare Pizza Dough on page 179 as directed except reduce the all-purpose flour that is stirred into the dough to ¾ to 1¼ cups and add ¾ cup yellow cornmeal after beating the flour and yeast mixture.

Cornmeal Pizza Dough
- ¾ **pound ground beef**
- 1 **cup chopped onion**
- 1 **8-ounce can tomato sauce**
- 1 **2¼-ounce can sliced pitted ripe olives, drained**
- 1 **1¼-ounce envelope taco seasoning mix**
- 2 **cups shredded cheddar cheese (8 ounces)**
- 2 **cups shredded lettuce**
- 2 **cups chopped tomatoes**
- 2 **medium avocados, seeded, peeled, and chopped**
- 1 **8-ounce carton dairy sour cream**
  Chili powder (optional)

Nutrition information per serving: 726 calories, 32 g protein, 56 g carbohydrate, 45 g fat (15 g saturated), 90 mg cholesterol, 1,274 mg sodium.

Easy Taco Pizza

Hearty Meat Pizza

Ground beef, pepperoni, and Canadian-style bacon top this scrumptious, stick-to-the-ribs pizza.

Pizza Dough

- ½ pound ground beef and/or bulk Italian sausage or pork sausage
- 1 cup chopped onion
- 1 15-ounce can pizza sauce or one 15½-ounce jar pizza sauce
- 1 3½-ounce package sliced pepperoni
- 1 cup cut-up Canadian-style bacon
- 1 cup chopped green pepper
- 2 cups shredded mozzarella cheese (8 ounces)
- ¼ cup grated Parmesan or Romano cheese

Prepare Pizza Dough. Grease two 11- to 13-inch pizza pans or baking sheets. On a lightly floured surface, roll each half of dough into a circle 1 inch larger than pizza pan. Transfer to pans. Build up edges slightly. Flute edges, if desired. Prick dough generously with a fork. Do not let rise. Bake in a 425° oven for 10 to 12 minutes or until lightly browned.

Meanwhile, in a large skillet cook ground beef and/or sausage and onion until meat is brown and onion is tender. Drain fat. Spread pizza sauce over hot crusts. Sprinkle with beef mixture. Top with pepperoni, Canadian-style bacon, and green pepper. Sprinkle with mozzarella and Parmesan or Romano cheese. Bake for 10 to 12 minutes more or until cheese melts and sauce is bubbly.

Makes 6 to 8 servings.

Pizza Dough: In a large bowl mix 1¼ cups all-purpose flour, 1 package active dry yeast, and ¼ teaspoon salt. Add 1 cup warm water and 2 tablespoons cooking oil. Beat with an electric mixer on low speed 30 seconds, scraping bowl constantly. Beat on high speed 3 minutes. Using a spoon, stir in as much of 1½ to 2 cups all-purpose flour as you can. Turn dough out onto a floured surface. Knead in enough of the remaining flour to make a moderately stiff dough that is smooth and elastic (6 to 8 minutes total). Divide dough in half. Cover and let rest.

Nutrition information per serving: 699 calories, 42 g protein, 57 g carbohydrate, 33 g fat (13 g saturated), 98 mg cholesterol, 1,427 mg sodium.

Reuben Pizza

All the ingredients of the ever-popular Reuben sandwich—corned beef, sauerkraut, and Swiss cheese—top this tasty pizza.

1 16-ounce loaf frozen whole wheat bread dough, thawed
½ cup Thousand Island salad dressing
2 cups shredded Swiss cheese (8 ounces)
6 ounces thinly sliced cooked corned beef
1 8-ounce can sauerkraut, rinsed and well drained
½ teaspoon caraway seed
   Dill pickle slices, chopped (optional)

On a lightly floured surface, roll bread dough into a 14-inch circle. Transfer to a greased 13-inch pizza pan. Build up edges slightly. Prick generously with a fork. Bake in a 375° oven for 20 to 25 minutes or until light brown.

Spread half of the salad dressing over hot crust. Sprinkle with half of the Swiss cheese. Arrange corned beef over cheese. Drizzle remaining salad dressing over corned beef. Top with sauerkraut and remaining Swiss cheese. Sprinkle with caraway seed.

Bake about 10 minutes more or until cheese melts and pizza is heated through. Top with chopped dill pickle, if desired.

Makes 6 servings.

Nutrition information per serving: 474 calories, 22 g protein, 38 g carbohydrate, 26 g fat (10 g saturated), 69 mg cholesterol, 724 mg sodium.

Southwestern Stuffed Pizza

For a doubly delicious taste, this robust pizza packs a zesty meat and corn filling between two crusts.

For filling, in a large skillet cook ground beef until brown. Drain fat. Stir in salsa, corn, cheese, olives, cilantro, the ¾ teaspoon cumin, and pepper. Set aside.

Prepare hot roll mix according to package directions, except stir the cornmeal and the ½ teaspoon cumin into the flour mixture and increase hot tap water to 1¼ cups. Turn dough out onto a lightly floured surface. Knead about 5 minutes or until smooth and elastic. Divide dough in half. Cover and let rest 5 minutes.

Meanwhile, grease an 11- to 13-inch pizza pan. Sprinkle with additional cornmeal, if desired. On a lightly floured surface, roll each half of dough into a circle 1 inch larger than pizza pan. Transfer one crust to pan. Spread meat mixture over dough.

Cut several slits in remaining crust. Place top crust on meat mixture. Trim and flute edges. Brush with beaten egg; sprinkle with additional cornmeal, if desired.

Bake in a 375° oven for 30 to 35 minutes or until the pastry is golden and pizza is heated through. If necessary to prevent overbrowning, cover pizza with foil after 20 minutes.

Makes 6 servings.

- 1½ pounds ground beef
- 1 12-ounce jar salsa
- 1 8-ounce can whole kernel corn, drained
- 1½ cups shredded cheddar cheese (6 ounces)
- ½ cup sliced pitted ripe olives
- 2 to 3 tablespoons snipped fresh cilantro
- ¾ teaspoon ground cumin
- ¼ teaspoon pepper
- 1 16-ounce package hot roll mix
- ¼ cup cornmeal
- ½ teaspoon ground cumin
- 1 beaten egg

Nutrition information per serving: 724 calories, 42 g protein, 69 g carbohydrate, 31 g fat (12 g saturated), 171 mg cholesterol, 1,305 mg sodium.

Prepare Garlic and Herb Pizza Dough. Grease two 11- to 13-inch pizza pans or baking sheets. On a lightly floured surface, roll each half of dough into a circle 1 inch larger than pizza pan. Transfer dough to pans. Build up edges slightly; flute edges, if desired. Prick generously with a fork. Do not let rise. Bake in a 425° oven for 10 to 12 minutes or until crust is lightly browned.

Meanwhile, rinse chicken; pat dry. Sprinkle both sides of chicken breast halves with lemon-pepper seasoning, pressing seasoning into the surface of the chicken. In a large skillet cook chicken in hot oil over medium heat for 8 to 10 minutes or until chicken is tender and no longer pink, turning often to brown evenly. Remove from skillet. Cut chicken into bite-size pieces.

Spread pizza sauce over hot crusts. Top with chicken pieces, green pepper strips, onion rings, mushrooms, and olives. Sprinkle with Parmesan or Romano cheese and basil. Sprinkle with Muenster cheese and Monterey Jack cheese. Bake about 12 minutes more or until cheese melts and sauce is bubbly.

Makes 6 servings.

Garlic and Herb Pizza Dough: Prepare Pizza Dough on page 179 as directed except add 2 teaspoons dried basil, oregano, or Italian seasoning, crushed, and 1 clove garlic, minced, with the dry ingredients.

Mozzarella is the cheese of choice for most pizzas, but other cheeses, such as Muenster, Monterey Jack, and cheddar, also can be used because of their good melting qualities.

Garlic and Herb Pizza Dough
- 1 **pound boneless skinless chicken breast halves**
- 2 **teaspoons lemon-pepper seasoning**
- 2 **tablespoons olive oil or cooking oil**
- 1 **15-ounce can pizza sauce or one 15½-ounce jar pizza sauce**
- 2 **small green peppers, cut into bite-size strips**
- 1 **medium red onion, sliced and separated into rings**
- 1 **cup sliced fresh mushrooms**
- 1 **2¼-ounce can sliced pitted ripe olives, drained**
- ¼ **cup grated Parmesan or Romano cheese**
- 2 **tablespoons snipped fresh basil or 2 teaspoons dried basil, crushed**
- 1 **cup shredded Muenster cheese (4 ounces)**
- 1 **cup shredded Monterey Jack cheese (4 ounces)**

Nutrition information per serving: 612 calories, 34 g protein, 55 g carbohydrate, 29 g fat (11 g saturated), 78 mg cholesterol, 1,196 mg sodium.

Cheesy Chicken-Vegetable Pizza

Drain artichoke hearts, reserving liquid. Cut artichoke hearts into bite-size pieces; set aside.

Rinse chicken; pat dry. Cut into cubes and set aside.

In a large skillet cook and stir zucchini and sweet pepper in hot oil until crisp-tender; remove from skillet. Add mushrooms and green onions to skillet. Cook and stir until just tender; remove from skillet.

In the same skillet cook chicken, half at a time, for 2 to 3 minutes or until no longer pink. Return all chicken to skillet. Stir in reserved artichoke hearts and liquid, tomatoes, olives, vinegar, garlic powder, seasoned salt, oregano, and basil. Combine cornstarch and water; add to skillet. Cook and stir until thickened and bubbly. Cook and stir 1 minute more. Return all vegetables to the skillet; stir until combined.

Place bread shell on a lightly greased baking sheet. Top with chicken mixture. Sprinkle with mozzarella cheese and Parmesan cheese.

Bake in a 425° oven for 10 to 12 minutes or until mozzarella cheese melts and pizza is heated through. Let stand 5 minutes before serving.

Makes 6 servings.

1	6½-ounce jar marinated artichoke hearts
¾	pound boneless skinless chicken breast halves
2	medium zucchini and/or yellow summer squash, thinly sliced
1	small red or green sweet pepper, chopped
1	tablespoon olive oil or cooking oil
1½	cups sliced fresh mushrooms
2	green onions, thinly sliced
2	plum or small common tomatoes, sliced
1	2¼-ounce can sliced pitted ripe olives
3	tablespoons vinegar
½	teaspoon garlic powder
½	teaspoon seasoned salt
½	teaspoon dried oregano, crushed
½	teaspoon dried basil, crushed
1	tablespoon cornstarch
1	tablespoon water
1	16-ounce package Boboli (12-inch Italian bread shell)
1½	cups shredded mozzarella cheese (6 ounces)
¼	cup grated Parmesan cheese

Nutrition information per serving: 491 calories, 34 g protein, 42 g carbohydrate, 23 g fat (7 g saturated), 71 mg cholesterol, 937 mg sodium.

Chicken-Artichoke Pizza

Pizza with Four Cheeses And Plum Tomatoes

Plum tomatoes are meaty, oval-shaped tomatoes with little juice and a mild, rich flavor. They also are called Italian or Roma tomatoes.

On a lightly floured surface, roll bread dough into a 14-inch circle. Transfer dough to a greased 13-inch pizza pan. Build up edges slightly. Prick generously with a fork. Bake in a 375° oven 20 to 25 minutes or until light brown.

Sprinkle chopped sweet peppers over hot crust. Top with mozzarella cheese, fontina cheese, Parmesan cheese, and feta cheese. Sprinkle parsley and basil over cheeses. Arrange tomato slices on top. In a small mixing bowl combine olive oil and garlic. Brush tomato slices with oil mixture.

Bake 15 to 20 minutes more or until cheeses melt and pizza is heated through. Let pizza stand for 5 minutes before serving.

Makes 6 servings.

1 16-ounce loaf frozen bread dough, thawed
2 large green and/or red sweet peppers, chopped (2 cups)
1 cup shredded mozzarella cheese (4 ounces)
¾ cup shredded fontina cheese (3 ounces)
½ cup grated Parmesan cheese (2 ounces)
½ cup crumbled feta cheese (2 ounces)
2 tablespoons snipped fresh parsley
1 tablespoon snipped fresh basil or 1 teaspoon dried basil, crushed
3 medium plum tomatoes or small tomatoes, thinly sliced
1 tablespoon olive oil or cooking oil
2 cloves garlic, minced

Nutrition information per serving: 379 calories, 19 g protein, 37 g carbohydrate, 17 g fat (6 g saturated), 42 mg cholesterol, 382 mg sodium.

Pepper-Bacon Burgers

The all-American burger just got spicy with the addition of serrano or jalapeño chili peppers.

In a large mixing bowl stir together egg, bread crumbs, bacon, serrano or jalapeño chili peppers, and milk. Add ground beef and mix well. Shape meat into four ¾-inch-thick patties.

Grill the patties, on an uncovered grill, directly over medium coals for 15 to 18 minutes or until no pink remains, turning once.

Meanwhile, in a small saucepan or skillet cook the chili pepper and onion in margarine or butter about 10 minutes or until onion is tender. Serve the burgers on lettuce-lined buns. Top the burgers with the pepper-onion mixture.

Makes 4 servings.

1 beaten egg

¼ cup fine dry bread crumbs

6 slices crisp cooked bacon, crumbled

4 to 6 serrano or 2 to 3 jalapeño chili peppers, seeded and finely chopped (3 tablespoons)

2 tablespoons milk

1 pound lean ground beef

1 Anaheim or mild green chili pepper, seeded and cut into rings

1 small onion, thinly sliced and separated into rings

2 tablespoons margarine or butter

4 lettuce leaves

4 kaiser rolls or hamburger buns, split and toasted

Nutrition information per serving: 550 calories, 32 g protein, 38 g carbohydrate, 29 g fat (9 g saturated), 132 g cholesterol, 733 mg sodium.

In a medium mixing bowl combine egg, celery, green sweet pepper, bread crumbs, onion, parsley, Worcestershire sauce, and salt. Add chicken; mix lightly but well. Shape into four 4-inch oval patties.

In a large skillet cook chicken patties in hot oil over medium heat for 10 to 12 minutes or until no longer pink, turning once. Spread each cut side of croissants with some of the Creamy Tarragon Sauce. Arrange a lettuce leaf and a chicken patty on bottom half of each croissant. Top each with a tomato slice and croissant top. Serve with any remaining Creamy Tarragon Sauce.

Makes 4 sandwiches.

Creamy Tarragon Sauce: In a small bowl combine ½ cup mayonnaise or salad dressing; 1 tablespoon finely chopped green onion; 1 teaspoon snipped parsley; ⅛ teaspoon dried tarragon, crushed; and a dash pepper. Stir to mix. Cover and chill until serving time. Makes ½ cup.

1   beaten egg
½   cup finely chopped celery
½   cup finely chopped green sweet pepper
⅓   cup fine dry seasoned bread crumbs
2   tablespoons finely chopped onion
1   tablespoon snipped parsley
1   teaspoon Worcestershire sauce
¼   teaspoon salt
1   pound ground raw chicken
2   tablespoons cooking oil
4   croissants, split lengthwise
    Creamy Tarragon Sauce
4   lettuce leaves
1   large tomato, sliced

Nutrition information per serving: 560 calories, 22 g protein, 23 g carbohydrate, 43 g fat (10 g saturated), 153 mg cholesterol, 610 mg sodium.

Chicken Patties on Croissants

Chicken Olive Calzones

Whether served plain or with spaghetti sauce, these sandwiches will be a family favorite.

For filling, in a medium bowl stir together chicken, Monterey Jack cheese, celery, ripe olives, basil, oregano, garlic powder, and pepper. Stir in soft-style cream cheese. Set aside.

For calzones, unroll pizza dough. On a lightly floured surface roll dough into a 15×10-inch rectangle. Cut into six 5-inch squares. Divide chicken-olive filling among the squares. Brush edges with water. Lift one corner and stretch dough over to the opposite corner. Seal edges of dough well with tines of a fork. Arrange calzones on a greased baking sheet. Prick tops with a fork. In a small bowl combine egg and 1 tablespoon water; brush over the calzones. Sprinkle with Parmesan cheese, if desired.

Bake in a 425° oven for 10 to 12 minutes or until golden brown. Let stand for 5 minutes before serving. Serve with heated spaghetti sauce, if desired.

Makes 6 calzones.

1 ½ cups chopped co(
     (8 ounces)
½ cup shredded Monterey Jack cheese
¼ cup chopped celery
¼ cup chopped pitted ripe olives
½ teaspoon dried basil, crushed
¼ teaspoon dried oregano, crushed
⅛ teaspoon garlic powder
⅛ teaspoon pepper
⅓ cup soft-style cream cheese with
    chives and onion
1 10-ounce package refrigerated
    pizza dough
1 beaten egg
1 tablespoon water
   Grated Parmesan cheese (optional)
   Spaghetti sauce (optional)

Nutrition information per calzone: 268 calories, 18 g protein, 19 g carbohydrate, 13 g fat (5 g saturated), 90 mg cholesterol, 320 mg sodium.

For filling, in a large bowl combine spinach, tuna, ricotta or cottage cheese, ½ cup Parmesan cheese, and garlic; set aside.

Unroll and separate the crescent dough into 4 rectangles. On an ungreased baking sheet or shallow baking pan, place rectangles together, overlapping edges slightly, to form a 14×10-inch rectangle. Firmly press edges and perforations together to seal.

Spread filling in a 3½-inch-wide strip, lengthwise down the center of dough. Top with provolone cheese, cutting cheese as necessary to cover the length of the filling.

Make cuts in dough at 1-inch intervals on both long sides of rectangle just to the edge of the filling. Fold dough strips diagonally over filling, overlapping strips and alternating from side to side to give a braided appearance.

Bake in a 375° oven for 18 to 20 minutes or until golden. Serve warm. If desired, serve with chopped tomatoes and additional grated Parmesan cheese.

Makes 4 servings.

Impressive, yet easy to make—an entertainer's delight. The filling can be made ahead of time and chilled to save last-minute preparation.

1   10-ounce package frozen chopped spinach, thawed and well drained
1   9¼-ounce can chunk white tuna (water pack), drained and flaked
1   cup ricotta cheese or cream-style cottage cheese, drained
½   cup grated Parmesan cheese
1   clove garlic, minced
1   package (8) refrigerated crescent rolls
3   thick slices provolone cheese (3 ounces)
    Chopped tomato (optional)
    Grated Parmesan cheese (optional)

Nutrition information per serving: 518 calories, 40 g protein, 29 g carbohydrate, 28 g fat (11 g saturated), 70 mg cholesterol, 1,245 mg sodium.

Tuna Spinach Braid

Cool and Creamy Cod Sandwiches

It's the horseradish mustard, a condiment often used to enhance the flavor of seafood, that puts the zip into this anything-but-ordinary sandwich.

12 ounces fresh or frozen cod fillets
½ stalk celery, finely chopped (¼ cup)
¼ cup mayonnaise or salad dressing
1 green onion, sliced (2 tablespoons)
1 to 2 tablespoons horseradish mustard
1 tablespoon lemon juice
¼ teaspoon ground black pepper
   Dash ground red pepper (optional)
4 individual French rolls
1 cup shredded lettuce (about
   2 ounces)

Thaw fish, if frozen. Rinse fish.

Pour ¾ inch of water into a large saucepan or Dutch oven. Place a steamer basket over the water. Bring to boiling. Gently lay fish in basket, cutting to fit if necessary. Cover and steam fish for 6 to 8 minutes or until fish flakes easily with a fork.

Remove fish from steamer basket. Pat fish dry with paper towels. Place fish in a large bowl. Using a fork, flake fish into small pieces. Stir in celery, mayonnaise or salad dressing, green onion, horseradish mustard, lemon juice, black pepper and red pepper, if desired. Mix until combined. Cover and chill 1 hour.

To assemble sandwiches, split French rolls horizontally. Place one-fourth of the shredded lettuce inside each bun. Top each with one-fourth of the chilled cod mixture.

Makes 4 servings.

Nutrition information per serving: 317 calories, 23 g protein, 25 g carbohydrate, 14 g fat (2 g saturated), 50 mg cholesterol, 418 mg sodium.

Clam and Bacon Bundles

Brushing the tops of the bundles with milk before baking makes them even more crispy and irresistibly golden brown.

In a large skillet cook bacon until crisp. Remove bacon, reserving 1 tablespoon drippings in skillet. Drain bacon on paper towels. Crumble; set aside.

For filling, cook broccoli and carrot in reserved drippings for 2 minutes. Add squash; cook for 1 minute more. Remove from heat. Stir in clams, cream cheese, salad dressing, and crumbled bacon. Set aside.

On a lightly floured surface, roll pizza dough to a 12×12-inch square. Cut dough into four 6-inch squares. Place ½ cup of the filling on one corner of each square. Moisten edges and fold opposite corner over filling. Press edges with tines of fork to seal. Brush bundles with milk. Sprinkle with sesame seed.

Place bundles on a greased baking sheet. Bake in a 400° oven about 20 minutes or until golden. Cool on a wire rack for 5 minutes. Serve warm.

Makes 4 servings.

2 slices bacon

¾ cup finely chopped broccoli (4 to 5 ounces)

1 medium shredded carrot (½ cup)

1 small yellow summer squash, chopped (1 cup)

2 6½-ounce cans chopped clams, drained

⅓ cup soft-style cream cheese with chives and onion

2 tablespoons creamy cucumber salad dressing

1 10-ounce package refrigerated pizza dough

1 tablespoon milk

1 tablespoon sesame seed

Nutrition information per serving: 390 calories, 23 g protein, 35 g carbohydrate, 18 g fat (5 g saturated), 57 mg cholesterol, 494 mg sodium.

Grilled Brie Sandwiches with Greens and Garlic

Instead of using all spinach for this deluxe grilled cheese sandwich, try a combination of half watercress and half spinach.

2 cloves garlic, minced
1 tablespoon olive oil or cooking oil
8 ounces fresh spinach, rinsed and stemmed (6 cups)
8 ounces cold Brie, cut into 1/8-inch slices
8 slices firm-textured whole grain bread
  Margarine or butter

In a large skillet cook garlic in hot oil for 30 seconds. Add spinach. Cook over medium heat, tossing until spinach begins to wilt; remove from heat. Set aside.

Divide the cheese among 4 slices of the bread. Top with spinach-garlic mixture. Cover with remaining bread slices. Lightly butter the outside of each sandwich.

In a large skillet cook half of the sandwiches over medium-low heat for 5 to 7 minutes or until golden brown. Turn sandwich and cook for 2 minutes more or until golden brown and cheese melts. Transfer to a warm oven. Repeat with remaining sandwiches.

Makes 4 servings.

Nutrition information per serving: 405 calories, 18 g protein, 25 g carbohydrate, 27 g fat (12 g saturated), 57 mg cholesterol, 771 mg sodium.

Couscous
Tacos

Couscous (KOOS-koos) is a quick-cooking grain made from ground semolina in the shape of very tiny beads. Look for it in the rice or pasta section of your supermarket or at specialty stores.

In a medium saucepan combine undrained stewed tomatoes, water, onion, and taco seasoning mix. Bring to a boil. Stir in couscous and tofu. Cover; remove from heat. Let stand for 5 minutes.

Spoon couscous mixture into taco shells. Top with lettuce and cheese. Serve with salsa.

Makes 5 servings.

1 14½-ounce can Mexican-style stewed tomatoes
1 cup water
¼ cup chopped onion
½ of a 1⅛- or 1¼-ounce envelope (5 teaspoons) taco seasoning mix
⅔ cup couscous
8 ounces firm or extra-firm tofu (fresh bean curd), drained and finely chopped
10 taco shells, warmed
1½ cups shredded lettuce
⅔ cup shredded cheddar cheese (about 3 ounces)
   Salsa

Nutrition information per serving: 365 calories, 18 g protein, 45 g carbohydrate, 15 g fat (4 g saturated), 16 mg cholesterol, 809 mg sodium.

Asparagus Egg Salad With Dill Dressing

Serve this knife-and-fork sandwich on your favorite toasted bagel or English muffin halves.

In a small saucepan cook asparagus or small broccoli flowerets in a small amount of boiling water for 3 minutes; drain and rinse under cold water. Drain well.

In a large mixing bowl combine the asparagus or broccoli, eggs, green onions, and pimiento.

For dressing, in a small mixing bowl stir together the mayonnaise or salad dressing, dill or dillweed, mustard, and vinegar or lemon juice. Stir dressing into egg mixture. Add salt and pepper to taste.

Arrange alfalfa sprouts on bagel or muffin halves. Spoon egg mixture over sprouts.

Makes 4 servings.

8 ounces fresh asparagus, cut into
    1-inch pieces, or 1 cup small
    broccoli flowerets
8 hard-cooked eggs, chopped
2 green onions, finely chopped (¼ cup)
2 tablespoons diced pimiento
¼ cup mayonnaise or salad dressing
1 teaspoon snipped fresh dill or
    ¼ teaspoon dried dillweed
1 teaspoon Dijon-style mustard
½ teaspoon white wine vinegar or
    lemon juice
    Salt
    Pepper
    Alfalfa sprouts
4 bagels or English muffins, split and
    toasted

Nutrition information per serving: 335 calories, 20 g protein, 34 g carbohydrate, 13 g fat (4 g saturated), 427 mg cholesterol, 494 mg sodium.

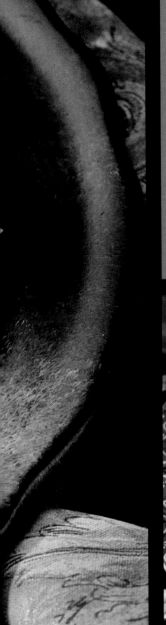

Cookouts Extraordinaire

209

Stir together catsup, pepper, rosemary, basil, garlic powder, and, if desired, cardamom. Coat both sides of steak with catsup mixture. Grill steak on an uncovered grill directly over medium coals for 6 minutes. Turn steak; grill for 8 to 12 minutes more or until desired doneness. Cut into serving-size pieces. Garnish with fresh rosemary, if desired.

Makes 6 servings.

Note: To grill by indirect heat, arrange preheated coals around a drip pan in a covered grill. Test for medium heat above pan. Place steak on grill over drip pan. Cover and grill for 20 to 24 minutes or until desired doneness, turning steak once.

 2 **tablespoons catsup**
$\frac{1}{2}$ **teaspoon coarsely ground pepper**
$1\frac{1}{2}$ **teaspoons snipped fresh rosemary or**
    $\frac{1}{2}$ **teaspoon dried rosemary, crushed**
$1\frac{1}{2}$ **teaspoons snipped fresh basil or $\frac{1}{2}$ teaspoon**
    dried basil, crushed
$\frac{1}{8}$ **teaspoon garlic powder**
$\frac{1}{8}$ **teaspoon ground cardamom (optional)**
 1 **$1\frac{1}{2}$-pound boneless beef sirloin steak,**
    cut 1 inch thick
    Fresh rosemary (optional)

Nutrition information per serving: 208 calories, 26 g protein, 2 g carbohydrate, 10 g fat (4 g saturated), 76 mg cholesterol, 124 mg sodium.

Herb-Pepper Sirloin Steak

Rib Eyes with Grilled Garlic

The garlic cloves mellow in flavor as they cook, making a delicious sauce for most any grilled meat or poultry. For an appetizer, spread the softened cloves over toasted slices of French bread.

1 whole head of garlic
2 tablespoons olive oil or cooking oil
1 tablespoon snipped fresh basil or
   ½ teaspoon dried basil, crushed
1 tablespoon snipped fresh rosemary or
   ½ teaspoon dried rosemary,
   crushed
2 12-ounce boneless rib eye steaks, cut
   1 inch thick
   Salt and pepper (optional)

Tear off a 24×18-inch piece of heavy foil. Fold in half crosswise. Trim to make a 12-inch square. Remove the papery outer layers from garlic head. Cut off and discard about ½ inch from top of garlic head to expose the garlic cloves. Place garlic head in center of foil. Bring the foil up around the garlic on all sides, forming a cup. Drizzle garlic with oil; sprinkle with basil and rosemary. Twist the ends of the foil to completely enclose the garlic in the foil.

Grill steaks and packet of garlic on an uncovered grill directly over medium coals 7 minutes. Turn steaks; grill for 5 to 8 minutes more or until desired doneness. Place steaks on serving platter. Open packet of garlic. Drizzle oil from packet over steak. Lift the softened cloves of garlic from head; spread over steak. Season with salt and pepper, if desired. Cut steak into serving-size pieces.

Makes 4 servings.

Note: To grill by indirect heat, arrange preheated coals around a drip pan in a covered grill. Test for medium heat above pan. Place steaks and garlic packet on grill over drip pan. Cover and grill for 18 to 24 minutes or until desired doneness, turning steaks once.

Nutrition information per serving: 366 calories, 34 g protein, 2 g carbohydrate, 24 g fat (8 g saturated), 100 mg cholesterol, 226 mg sodium.

Grilled Stuffed Meat Loaf

The indirect grilling method and a square of heavy foil make easy work of grilling a meat loaf.

1 tablespoon margarine or butter
2 cups sliced fresh mushrooms
1 medium onion, thinly sliced
2 tablespoons snipped parsley
½ cup rolled oats
⅓ cup milk
¾ teaspoon salt
¼ teaspoon pepper
1 beaten egg
1½ pounds lean ground beef
2 tablespoons catsup
1 teaspoon prepared mustard

In a small skillet heat margarine or butter over medium heat until melted. Add mushrooms and onion; cook over medium heat about 5 minutes or until vegetables are tender. Stir in parsley. Cool slightly.

Stir together rolled oats, milk, salt, pepper, and egg. Add ground beef and mix well. Place on waxed paper and flatten to a 12×8-inch rectangle. Spoon mushroom and onion mixture evenly onto meat. Roll up, starting with 8-inch end. Seal seam and ends by pinching together. Stir together catsup and mustard.

Arrange preheated coals around a drip pan in a covered grill. Test for medium-low heat above pan. Tear off a 24×18-inch piece of heavy foil. Fold in half to make a double thickness of foil that measures 18×12 inches. Trim to make a 12-inch square. Cut several slits in the foil square. Place foil on grill over drip pan. Place meat loaf on foil. Cover and grill for 50 to 60 minutes or until no pink remains in meat, brushing with catsup mixture during the last 5 minutes of grilling. Remove meat loaf from the grill and cover with foil. Let stand 15 minutes before slicing.

Makes 6 servings.

Nutrition information per serving: 296 calories, 25 g protein, 9 g carbohydrate, 17 g fat (6 g saturated), 107 mg cholesterol, 445 mg sodium.

For onions, tear a 36×18-inch piece of heavy foil. Fold in half to make a double thickness of foil that measures 18×18 inches. Place onions in the center of the foil. Combine melted margarine, mustard, and honey. Drizzle over onions. Bring up two opposite edges of foil and seal with double fold. Then fold remaining ends to completely enclose onion mixture, leaving space for steam to build. Place packet on an uncovered grill directly over medium coals for 15 minutes.

Meanwhile, in a medium bowl combine ground beef, salt, and pepper; mix well. Shape mixture into four ¾-inch-thick patties. Add patties to grill. Grill patties and onions for 5 minutes. Turn patties. Grill for 8 to 10 minutes more or until no pink remains in meat and onions are tender. To serve, toast both sides of Texas toast on grill. Top each slice of Texas toast with a lettuce leaf, a burger, a tomato slice, and one-fourth of the onions. Sprinkle with fresh ground pepper, if desired.

Makes 4 servings.

Note: To grill by indirect heat, arrange preheated coals around a drip pan in a covered grill. Test for medium heat above pan. Place patties on grill over drip pan. Place onion packet directly over medium-hot coals. Cover and grill for 20 to 24 minutes or until no pink remains in burgers and onions are very tender, turning patties once halfway through grilling time.

A honey and mustard sauce glazes the onion slices as they cook in a foil packet alongside these delicious burgers. For optimal sweetness, select Vidalia or Walla Walla onions.

2 **large sweet onions, sliced (12 to 16 ounces)**
2 **tablespoons margarine or butter, melted**
2 **teaspoons dry mustard**
2 **teaspoons honey**
1 **pound lean ground beef**
¼ **teaspoon salt**
⅛ **teaspoon pepper**
4 **slices Texas toast**
4 **lettuce leaves**
4 **tomato slices**
Fresh ground pepper (optional)

Nutrition information per serving: 421 calories, 27 g protein, 31 g carbohydrate, 22 g fat (7 g saturated), 70 mg cholesterol, 527 mg sodium.

Sweet Onion Burgers

For sauce, in a medium skillet cook onion in oil over medium heat about 4 minutes until onion is tender. Stir in catsup, orange juice, brown sugar, chili powder, and gingerroot. Continue cooking over medium heat for about 5 minutes or until thickened slightly. Trim fat from meat. Cut the ribs into serving-size pieces.

Arrange preheated coals around a drip pan in a covered grill. Test for medium heat above pan. Place ribs on grill over drip pan. Cover and grill for $1\frac{1}{4}$ to $1\frac{1}{2}$ hours or until ribs are tender and no pink remains, brushing with sauce the last 10 minutes of grilling.

Makes 6 servings.

1 **medium onion, chopped ($\frac{1}{2}$ cup)**
1 **tablespoon cooking oil**
$\frac{1}{3}$ **cup catsup**
2 **tablespoons orange juice**
1 **tablespoon brown sugar**
1 **teaspoon chili powder**
$\frac{1}{2}$ **teaspoon grated gingerroot**
4 **pounds pork loin back ribs or meaty spareribs**

Nutrition information per serving: 313 calories, 19 g protein, 8 g carbohydrate, 22 g fat (8 g saturated), 79 mg cholesterol, 245 mg sodium.

Down-Home Ribs

Fruit-Stuffed Pork Chops

Chunks of sweet apple and snips of tangy apricot fill these marmalade-glazed chops.

Combine apple, apricots, raisins, chives, and cardamom. Trim fat from meat. Season with salt and pepper, if desired. Make a pocket in each chop by cutting horizontally into the chop from the fat side almost to the bone. Spoon fruit mixture into each pocket. If necessary, securely fasten the opening with water-soaked wooden toothpicks. Combine marmalade and sherry or orange juice.

Arrange preheated coals around a drip pan in a covered grill. Test for medium heat above pan. Place chops on grill over drip pan. Cover and grill for 35 to 40 minutes or until juices run clear, brushing occasionally with marmalade mixture during the last 10 minutes of grilling.

Makes 6 servings.

1   medium apple, cored and chopped
$\frac{1}{4}$ cup snipped dried apricots
$\frac{1}{4}$ cup raisins
1   tablespoon snipped fresh chives or
     1 teaspoon dried chives
$\frac{1}{8}$ teaspoon ground cardamom
6   pork loin or rib chops, cut $1\frac{1}{4}$ inches
     thick (about 3 pounds total)
     Salt and pepper (optional)
2   tablespoons orange marmalade
1   tablespoon dry sherry or orange juice

Nutrition information per serving: 237 calories, 20 g protein, 15 g carbohydrate, 11 g fat (4 g saturated), 66 mg cholesterol, 54 mg sodium.

Mustardy Brats with Sauerkraut

A sweet, yet puckery sauerkraut relish tops these spicy brats.

1 tablespoon margarine or butter
½ cup chopped green sweet pepper
1 small onion, chopped (⅓ cup)
2 tablespoons brown sugar
1 teaspoon prepared mustard
½ teaspoon caraway seed
1 cup drained sauerkraut
6 fresh bratwurst (1¼ to 1½ pounds)
6 hoagie buns, split

In a small skillet heat margarine or butter over medium heat until melted. Add green pepper and onion. Cook over medium heat about 5 minutes or until tender. Stir in brown sugar, mustard, and caraway seed. Add sauerkraut; toss to mix. Tear off a 36×18-inch piece of heavy foil. Fold in half to make a double thickness of foil that measures 18×18 inches. Place sauerkraut mixture in center of foil. Bring up two opposite edges of foil and seal with double fold. Then fold remaining ends to completely enclose sauerkraut mixture, leaving space for steam to build. Prick the bratwurst in several places with a fork or the tip of a sharp knife.

Arrange preheated coals around a drip pan in a covered grill. Test for medium heat above the pan. Place bratwurst and the foil packet on grill over pan. Cover and grill for 20 to 25 minutes or until bratwurst juices run clear, turning bratwurst over once. To serve, toast cut sides of buns on grill. Serve bratwurst in the buns and top with sauerkraut mixture.

Makes 6 servings.

Nutrition information per serving: 663 calories, 22 g protein, 83 g carbohydrate, 27 g fat (10 g saturated), 46 mg cholesterol, 1,472 mg sodium.

Grecian
Kabobs

For marinade, combine oil, lemon juice, chives, oregano, water, and garlic. Trim fat from meat; place meat in plastic bag set into a shallow dish. Add marinade; seal bag. Turn meat to coat well. Chill for 4 to 24 hours, turning meat occasionally.

Meanwhile, cook onion wedges in a small amount of boiling water for 3 minutes. Drain and cool slightly.

Remove meat from bag, reserving marinade. On eight short or four long skewers, alternately thread lamb or pork cubes with onion, peppers, and mushrooms, leaving about ¼ inch space between each.

Grill kabobs on an uncovered grill directly over medium coals for 12 to 14 minutes or until desired doneness, turning once and brushing with reserved marinade. Serve over hot cooked couscous and garnish with fresh oregano, if desired.

Makes 4 servings.

Note: To grill by indirect heat, arrange preheated coals around a drip pan. Test for medium heat above pan. Place skewers on grill over drip pan. Cover and grill for 16 to 18 minutes or until desired doneness, brushing with reserved marinade halfway through cooking time.

Nutrition information per serving: 177 calories, 19 g protein, 5 g carbohydrate, 9 g fat (3 g saturated), 57 mg cholesterol, 46 mg sodium.

2 **tablespoons olive oil or cooking oil**

2 **tablespoons lemon juice**

1 **tablespoon snipped fresh chives or**
   1 **teaspoon dried chives**

1 **tablespoon snipped fresh oregano or**
   1 **teaspoon dried oregano, crushed**

1 **tablespoon water**

1 **clove garlic, minced**

1 **pound lean boneless lamb or pork,**
   cut into 1-inch cubes

1 **medium red onion, cut into wedges**

1 **medium green sweet pepper, cut into**
   1-inch squares

2 **cups fresh mushrooms**
   Hot cooked couscous (optional)
   Fresh oregano (optional)

All-American
Barbecued
Chicken

Make it an all-American barbecue with roasted corn on the cob and macaroni salad bathed in a light vinaigrette.

For sauce, in a saucepan cook onion in hot oil until onion is tender. Stir in catsup, water, vinegar, brown sugar, Worcestershire sauce, and bottled hot pepper sauce. Bring to boiling; reduce heat. Simmer, uncovered, about 15 minutes or to desired consistency.

Meanwhile, rinse chicken; pat dry with paper towels. Break wing, hip, and drumstick joints so pieces lie flat. Twist wing tips under back. Grill chicken, skin side down, on an uncovered grill directly over medium coals for 20 minutes. Turn chicken; grill for 15 to 20 minutes more or until chicken is tender and no longer pink. (Or, place chicken on the unheated rack of a broiler pan. Broil 5 to 6 inches from the heat for 28 to 32 minutes, turning once.) Brush with sauce during the last 10 minutes of grilling or broiling. Heat remaining sauce until bubbly; pass with chicken.

Makes 4 to 6 servings.

1 **medium onion, finely chopped (½ cup)**
1 **tablespoon cooking oil**
1 **cup catsup**
½ **cup water**
¼ **cup vinegar**
2 **to 3 tablespoons brown sugar**
2 **tablespoons Worcestershire sauce**
2 **dashes bottled hot pepper sauce**
1 **2½- to 3-pound broiler-fryer chicken, quartered**

Nutrition information per serving: 407 calories, 32 g protein, 29 g carbohydrate, 19 g fat (5 g saturated), 98 mg cholesterol, 996 mg sodium.

Herb-Stuffed Chicken Breasts

For direct grilling, cook the chicken with the skin on to keep the meat moist and juicy (you can remove the skin before eating, if you like). For indirect grilling, you can remove the skin before cooking.

1 **3-ounce package cream cheese, softened**
2 **tablespoons snipped fresh basil leaves**
1 **tablespoon snipped fresh chives**
1 **clove garlic, minced**
6 **chicken breast halves (about 2¼ pounds total)**
2 **tablespoons olive oil or cooking oil**
1 **tablespoon lemon or lime juice**
1 **tablespoon water**
  Fresh chives (optional)
  Fresh basil (optional)

For the stuffing, in a small bowl stir together cream cheese, basil, chives, and garlic.

Skin chicken, if desired. Rinse chicken; pat dry with paper towels. Cut a slit horizontally in each chicken breast to make a 3-inch-square pocket. Insert a rounded tablespoon of stuffing into each slit. Fasten slit closed with water-soaked wooden toothpicks. Combine oil, lemon or lime juice, and water.

Grill chicken, bone side up, on an uncovered grill directly over medium coals for 15 minutes, brushing occasionally with oil mixture. Turn chicken and grill for 20 to 30 minutes more or until chicken is tender and no longer pink, brushing occasionally with oil mixture. Garnish with fresh chives and basil, if desired.

Makes 6 servings.

Note: To grill by indirect heat, arrange preheated coals around a drip pan in a covered grill. Test for medium heat above the pan. Place chicken, bone side down, on grill over drip pan. Cover and grill for 50 to 60 minutes or until chicken is tender and no longer pink, brushing occasionally with oil mixture.

Nutrition information per serving: 273 calories, 29 g protein, 1 g carbohydrate, 17 g fat (6 g saturated), 94 mg cholesterol, 108 mg sodium.

For marinade, combine soy sauce, lemon juice, garlic, gingerroot, and mustard. Rinse chicken; pat dry with paper towels. Cut chicken into 1-inch pieces; place in plastic bag set into a shallow dish. Add marinade; seal bag. Turn chicken to coat well. Chill for 2 to 24 hours, turning chicken occasionally.

Remove chicken from bag, reserving marinade. Cut green and red peppers into 1-inch pieces. On six 12-inch metal skewers alternately thread chicken, pineapple, green pepper, and red pepper. Grill on uncovered grill directly over medium coals for 5 minutes. Brush with marinade; turn skewers and grill for 7 to 9 minutes more or until chicken is tender and no longer pink. Serve kabobs over hot cooked rice and garnish with green onion brushes, if desired.

Makes 6 servings.

Note: To grill by indirect heat, arrange preheated coals around a drip pan in a covered grill. Test for medium heat above pan. Place skewers on grill over drip pan. Cover and grill for 16 to 18 minutes or until chicken is tender and no longer pink, brushing occasionally with marinade up to the last 5 minutes of grilling.

¼ **cup soy sauce**

2 **tablespoons lemon juice**

2 **cloves garlic, minced**

1 **teaspoon grated fresh gingerroot or**
 ⅛ **teaspoon ground ginger**

⅛ **teaspoon dry mustard**

1 **pound boneless, skinless chicken breasts or thighs**

1 **medium green sweet pepper**

1 **medium red sweet pepper**

1 **cup fresh pineapple chunks or one 8-ounce can pineapple chunks, drained**

Hot cooked rice (optional)

Green onion brushes (optional)

Nutrition information per serving: 110 calories, 15 g protein, 7 g carbohydrate, 2 g fat (1 g saturated), 40 mg cholesterol, 723 mg sodium.

Polynesian Chicken Kabobs

Grilled Turkey Burgers

Who says beef has to make the all-American burger? We gave the classic burger a makeover by using ground turkey, glazing it with orange marmalade, and serving it on rye or wheat buns.

1 beaten egg

⅓ cup fine dry bread crumbs

¼ cup finely chopped green sweet pepper

2 green onions, finely chopped

2 tablespoons milk

½ teaspoon salt

⅛ teaspoon pepper

1 pound ground raw turkey

2 tablespoons orange marmalade

5 rye or wheat sandwich buns, split

Shredded lettuce (optional)

Tomato slices, halved (optional)

Onion slices (optional)

In large mixing bowl combine egg, bread crumbs, green pepper, onions, milk, salt, and pepper. Add turkey and mix well. Shape mixture into five ¾-inch-thick patties.

Grill patties on an uncovered grill directly over medium coals for 6 minutes. Turn patties and brush with marmalade. Grill for 8 to 12 minutes more or until no pink remains. Toast cut sides of buns on grill. Serve patties in buns and, if desired, with lettuce, tomato, and onion.

Makes 5 servings.

Note: To grill by indirect heat, arrange preheated coals around a drip pan in a covered grill. Test for medium heat above pan. Place patties on grill over drip pan. Cover and grill for 20 to 24 minutes or until no pink remains, turning patties once halfway through grilling time and brushing with marmalade.

Nutrition information per serving: 289 calories, 17 g protein, 30 g carbohydrate, 11 g fat (2 g saturated), 77 mg cholesterol, 396 mg sodium.

Apricot-Stuffed Turkey Breast

Here's a tip from our Test Kitchen: Use kitchen shears to snip the dried apricots. It's easier, faster, and less messy than a knife and cutting board.

Remove bone from turkey breast. Rinse turkey; pat dry with paper towels. Cut a horizontal slit into thickest part of turkey breast to form a 5×4-inch pocket. Set aside.

In a medium mixing bowl combine bread crumbs, apricots, pecans, margarine or butter, sherry or apple juice, rosemary, and garlic salt. Spoon stuffing into pocket. Securely fasten opening with water-soaked wooden toothpicks or tie with heavy string. Stir together mustard and oil; set aside.

Arrange preheated coals around a drip pan in a covered grill. Test for medium heat above pan. Place turkey on grill over drip pan. Cover and grill for 1 to 1¼ hours or until turkey is no longer pink, brushing with mustard mixture during the last 15 minutes. Remove turkey from grill and cover with foil. Let stand for 15 minutes before slicing.

Makes 8 servings.

1   2- to 2½-pound turkey breast half
      with skin and bone
1½ cups soft bread crumbs (2 slices)
½   cup snipped dried apricots
¼   cup chopped toasted pecans
2   tablespoons margarine or butter,
      melted
2   tablespoons dry sherry or apple juice
¼   teaspoon dried rosemary, crushed
¼   teaspoon garlic salt
1   tablespoon Dijon-style mustard
1   tablespoon olive oil

Nutrition information per serving: 208 calories, 21 g protein, 8 g carbohydrate, 9 g total fat (2 g saturated fat), 46 mg cholesterol, 231 mg sodium.

Turkey Tenderloins with Honey-Lemon Sauce

In a hurry? These turkey tenderloins can be ready in about 30 minutes. Be sure to light the coals as your first step—they'll need 20 to 30 minutes before they are ready for grilling.

Finely shred enough peel from the lemon to make 1 teaspoon. Cut lemon in half. Squeeze one half to obtain 2 tablespoons juice; set peel and juice aside. Rinse turkey; pat dry with paper towels. Rub and squeeze cut surface of remaining lemon half over turkey.

For sauce, in a small saucepan combine water, honey, catsup, cornstarch, bouillon, the 1 teaspoon lemon peel, and the 2 tablespoons lemon juice. Cook and stir over medium heat until sauce thickens and bubbles; cook and stir 2 minutes more. Keep warm.

Grill turkey on an uncovered grill directly over medium coals for 5 minutes. Turn turkey; grill for 7 to 10 minutes more or until turkey is tender and no longer pink. Spoon sauce over turkey. Serve with lemon wedges, if desired.

Makes 4 servings.

Note: To grill by indirect heat, arrange preheated coals around a drip pan in a covered grill. Test for medium heat above pan. Place turkey on grill over drip pan. Cover and grill for 15 to 18 minutes or until turkey is tender and no longer pink.

1 **large lemon**
⅓ **cup water**
3 **tablespoons honey**
1 **tablespoon catsup**
2 **teaspoons cornstarch**
1 **teaspoon instant chicken bouillon granules**
4 **turkey breast tenderloin steaks (about 1 pound total)**
  Lemon wedges (optional)

Nutrition information per serving: 175 calories, 22 g protein, 16 g carbohydrate, 2 g fat (1 g saturated), 50 mg cholesterol, 314 mg sodium.

Leftovers? Combine flaked chilled salmon with leftover sauce for delicious salmon salad or sandwich filling.

Thaw fish, if frozen.

For sauce, in a small bowl combine cucumber, mayonnaise or salad dressing, yogurt, and horseradish. Cover and chill until serving time. Combine margarine or butter and dill; set aside.

Grill salmon on the greased rack of an uncovered grill directly over medium coals for 8 to 12 minutes or just until fish begins to flake easily, turning once and brushing occasionally with dill mixture. Serve salmon with sauce. If desired, garnish with cucumber slices and fresh dill.

Makes 4 servings.

Note: To grill by indirect heat, arrange preheated coals around a drip pan in a covered grill. Test for medium heat above pan. Place salmon steaks on greased grill over drip pan. Cover and grill for 8 to 12 minutes or just until fish begins to flake easily, turning once and brushing occasionally with dill mixture.

4 **6-ounce fresh or frozen salmon steaks, cut 1 inch thick**
⅓ **cup finely chopped cucumber**
2 **tablespoons mayonnaise or salad dressing**
2 **tablespoons plain yogurt**
1 **teaspoon prepared horseradish**
1 **tablespoon margarine or butter, melted**
1 **teaspoon snipped fresh dill or ¼ teaspoon dried dillweed**
   Cucumber slices, halved (optional)
   Fresh dill (optional)

Nutrition information per serving: 237 calories, 25 g protein, 1 g carbohydrate, 14 g fat (3 g saturated), 35 mg cholesterol, 193 mg sodium.

Salmon with Cucumber-Horseradish Sauce

To serve grilled sweet pepper strips with the swordfish, place the strips over hot coals the last 5 minutes of grilling.

Thaw fish, if frozen.

For chili salsa, in a small bowl stir together tomato, chili sauce, salsa, cilantro, and cumin. Cover and chill until serving time.

Brush both sides of fish with oil. Grill fish steaks on the greased rack of an uncovered grill directly over medium coals for 8 to 12 minutes or just until fish begins to flake easily, turning once and brushing occasionally with oil. Serve with chili salsa.

Makes 4 servings.

Note: To grill by indirect heat, arrange preheated coals around a drip pan in a covered grill. Test for medium heat above pan. Place fish on the greased grill rack over drip pan. Cover and grill for 8 to 12 minutes or just until fish begins to flake easily, brushing occasionally with oil.

4	6-ounce fresh or frozen swordfish steaks, cut 1 inch thick
1	small tomato, chopped
¼	cup chili sauce
¼	cup salsa
2	tablespoons snipped fresh cilantro
¼	teaspoon ground cumin
1	tablespoon olive oil or cooking oil

Nutrition information per serving: 263 calories, 35 g protein, 6 g carbohydrate, 11 g fat (2 g saturated), 67 mg cholesterol, 412 mg sodium.

Swordfish with Chili Salsa

Thaw shrimp, if frozen.

For marinade, combine pineapple juice concentrate, jalapeño pepper, garlic, gingerroot, and crushed red pepper. Peel and devein shrimp. Place shrimp in a plastic bag set into a shallow dish. Add marinade; seal bag. Turn shrimp to coat well. Chill for 1 to 2 hours, turning shrimp once.

Remove shrimp from bag, reserving marinade. Thread shrimp on five metal skewers. Grill on an uncovered grill directly over medium coals for 6 to 8 minutes or until shrimp turn opaque, turning skewers once and brushing with marinade.

Makes 5 servings.

Note: To grill by indirect heat, arrange preheated coals around a drip pan in a covered grill. Test for medium heat above pan. Place skewers on grill over drip pan. Cover and grill for 8 to 10 minutes or until shrimp turn opaque, brushing occasionally with marinade.

For a tangy accompaniment to the peppery shrimp, add fresh pineapple wedges to the grill alongside the shrimp during the last 5 minutes of cooking.

1½ **pounds fresh or frozen large shrimp in shells**
½ **cup frozen pineapple juice concentrate, thawed**
1 **to 2 tablespoons finely chopped jalapeño peppers**
1 **clove garlic, minced**
1 **teaspoon grated gingerroot or**
⅛ **teaspoon ground ginger**
¼ **teaspoon crushed red pepper**

Nutrition information per serving: 133 calories, 17 g protein, 13 g carbohydrate, 1 g fat (0 g saturated), 157 mg cholesterol, 181 mg sodium.

Spicy Shrimp on Skewers

Cook broccoli and zucchini in enough boiling water to cover for 2 minutes. Drain and rinse immediately in cold water. Set aside.

Lightly grease an 11- to 13-inch pizza pan. Unroll pizza dough and transfer to greased pan, pressing out dough with your hands. Build up edges slightly. Prick generously with a fork.

Place pizza pan on the grill rack directly over medium coals. Cover grill and grill for 5 minutes. Carefully remove pan from grill.

Spread pizza sauce or pesto over hot crust. Top with cooked vegetables, shrimp, and pepperoni. Sprinkle with mozzarella cheese. Return pizza to grill rack. Grill, covered, about 10 minutes more or until cheese melts and pizza is heated through, checking occasionally to make sure crust doesn't overbrown.

Makes 6 servings.

1   **cup broccoli flowerets**
1   **small zucchini, quartered lengthwise and sliced**
1   **10-ounce package refrigerated pizza dough**
¾   **cup pizza sauce or ⅓ cup purchased pesto**
¾   **pound peeled, cooked shrimp**
½   **of a 3½-ounce package sliced pepperoni**
1½ **cups shredded mozzarella cheese (6 ounces)**

Nutrition information per serving: 289 calories, 24 g protein, 23 g carbohydrate, 11 g fat (4 g saturated), 127 mg cholesterol, 726 mg sodium.

Grilled Shrimp and Pepperoni Pizza

Something Savory on the Side

Hot-Style
Garlic Spinach

Pour cooking oil and chili oil into a wok or 12-inch skillet. (Add more cooking oil as necessary during cooking.) Preheat over medium-high heat. Stir-fry garlic in hot oil for 15 seconds.

Add sweet pepper; stir-fry for 2 minutes. Add spinach; stir-fry for 2 to 3 minutes or just until spinach is wilted. (Add 1 tablespoon water if spinach mixture is dry.)

Stir in fish sauce or soy sauce and pepper. Serve immediately with a slotted spoon.

Makes 3 or 4 servings.

1 **tablespoon cooking oil**

¼ **teaspoon chili oil**

4 **cloves garlic, minced**

1 **small red or yellow sweet pepper, cut into thin strips (¾ cup)**

1 **10-ounce package cleaned fresh spinach, torn (8 cups)**

1½ **teaspoons fish sauce or soy sauce**

⅛ **teaspoon pepper**

Nutrition information per serving: 91 *calories,* 5 *g protein,* 9 *g carbohydrate,* 6 *g fat (*1 *g saturated),* 0 *mg cholesterol,* 212 *mg sodium.*

Sesame Vegetables

Soy sauce, ginger, and garlic are frequently used in concert to flavor many Chinese-style dishes. In this dish, the addition of toasted sesame oil and sesame seeds gives the vegetables an added flavor boost.

For sauce, in a small bowl stir together soy sauce, sugar, and sesame oil. Set aside.

Pour cooking oil into a wok or 12-inch skillet. (Add more oil as necessary during cooking.) Preheat over medium-high heat. Stir-fry gingerroot and garlic in hot oil for 15 seconds. Add broccoli and asparagus; stir-fry about 4 minutes or until vegetables are crisp-tender. Remove broccoli mixture from the wok.

Add squash, mushrooms, and sesame seed to the hot wok; stir-fry for 2 to 3 minutes or until crisp-tender. Return broccoli mixture to the wok. Add green onions.

Pour sauce over vegetables. Cook and stir 1 to 2 minutes more or until heated through. Serve immediately.

Makes 4 to 6 servings.

2 **tablespoons soy sauce**
½ **teaspoon sugar**
½ **teaspoon toasted sesame oil**
1 **tablespoon cooking oil**
1 **teaspoon grated gingerroot**
2 **cloves garlic, minced**
2 **cups broccoli flowerets**
12 **ounces fresh asparagus, woody ends trimmed, and bias-cut into 1-inch pieces (2 cups)**
2 **small yellow summer squash, halved lengthwise and sliced ¼ inch thick (2 cups)**
4 **ounces fresh mushrooms, sliced (1½ cups)**
1 **tablespoon sesame seed**
2 **green onions, sliced (¼ cup)**

Nutrition information per serving: 117 calories, 6 g protein, 14 g carbohydrate, 6 g fat (1 g saturated), 0 mg cholesterol, 540 mg sodium.

Pour cooking oil into a wok or large skillet. (Add more oil as necessary during cooking.) Preheat over medium-high heat. Stir-fry zucchini and yellow squash in hot oil for 3 to 4 minutes or until crisp-tender. Remove vegetables from the wok.

Add broccoli, basil, oregano, salt, and pepper to the hot wok. Stir-fry for 2 to 3 minutes or until crisp-tender.

Return cooked zucchini and yellow squash to the wok. Add tomato and butter or margarine. Stir-fry just until butter is melted. Serve immediately.

Makes 4 to 6 servings.

This simple dish enhances the natural goodness of summer vegetables with a generous sprinkling of fresh, fragrant herbs and just a dab of butter.

1 **tablespoon cooking oil**
2 **small zucchini, thinly bias-sliced (2 cups)**
2 **small yellow summer squash, thinly bias-sliced (2 cups)**
2 **cups broccoli flowerets**
2 **teaspoons snipped fresh basil or ¾ teaspoon dried basil, crushed**
2 **teaspoons snipped fresh oregano or ¾ teaspoon dried oregano, crushed**
¼ **teaspoon salt**
⅛ **teaspoon pepper**
1 **medium tomato, chopped**
1 **tablespoon butter or margarine**

Nutrition information per serving: 97 calories, 3 g protein, 8 g carbohydrate, 7 g fat (2 g saturated), 8 mg cholesterol, 187 mg sodium.

Butter-Glazed
Summer Vegetables

Leek-Gruyère Cream Soup

The leek is a member of the onion family that resembles an overgrown green onion with overlapping wide, green leaves; a fat, white stalk; and shaggy roots at the bulb end. Leeks have a subtle onion flavor.

6 cups chicken broth
4 cups sliced leeks
1 cup sliced fresh mushrooms
1 teaspoon fines herbes, crushed
½ teaspoon white pepper
⅓ cup all-purpose flour
1½ cups shredded process Gruyère
      cheese (6 ounces)
2 tablespoons snipped fresh parsley
1 cup whipping cream
   Thinly sliced leeks (optional)

In a large kettle or Dutch oven combine 4 cups of the chicken broth, leeks, mushrooms, fines herbes, and pepper. Bring to boiling. Reduce heat and simmer, covered, for 10 to 15 minutes or until leeks are tender. Cool slightly.

Place one-third of the leek mixture in a blender container or food processor bowl. Cover and blend or process until smooth. Repeat with remaining leek mixture. Return all of the smooth leek mixture to the kettle or Dutch oven; stir in 1 cup of the remaining chicken broth.

Combine the remaining 1 cup of the chicken broth and the flour until smooth. Stir into hot broth mixture along with shredded cheese and parsley. Cook and stir until slightly thickened and bubbly and cheese melts. Stir in whipping cream; heat through.

If desired, garnish with additional sliced leeks.

Makes 8 servings.

Nutrition information per serving: 193 calories, 7 g protein, 11 g carbohydrate, 14 g fat (8 g saturated), 47 mg cholesterol, 618 mg sodium.

Oriental Hot-and-Sour Soup

This Chinese specialty is delightfully peppery and vinegary.

Thaw shrimp, if frozen. In a large saucepan or Dutch oven combine chicken broth, mushrooms (if desired), rice vinegar or white vinegar, soy sauce, sugar, gingerroot, and pepper. Bring to boiling. Reduce heat and simmer, covered, for 2 minutes.

Add shrimp and tofu. Simmer, covered, for 1 minute more. Stir together cornstarch and cold water. Stir into chicken broth mixture along with pea pods. Cook and stir until slightly thickened and bubbly. Cook and stir for 2 minutes more. Pour the egg into the soup in a steady stream while stirring 2 or 3 times to create shreds. Remove from heat. Stir in green onion.

Makes 6 servings.

8 ounces fresh or frozen peeled and deveined shrimp

3½ cups chicken broth

1 7-ounce jar whole straw mushrooms, drained and halved lengthwise (optional)

¼ cup rice vinegar or white vinegar

2 tablespoons soy sauce

1 teaspoon sugar

1 teaspoon grated gingerroot

½ teaspoon pepper

4 ounces tofu (fresh bean curd), cut into bite-size pieces

1 tablespoon cornstarch

1 tablespoon cold water

1 cup fresh pea pods, halved crosswise, or ½ of a 6-ounce package frozen pea pods, thawed and halved crosswise

1 beaten egg

2 tablespoons thinly sliced green onion

Nutrition information per serving: 117 calories, 14 g protein, 7 g carbohydrate, 4 g fat (1 g saturated), 94 mg cholesterol, 877 mg sodium.

Strawberry
Spinach Salad

For a quick-to-fix main dish, toss about a pound of chopped cooked chicken or turkey with the greens, berries, and asparagus.

1 pound asparagus spears

¼ cup poppy seed or Italian salad dressing

1 teaspoon finely shredded orange peel

1 tablespoon orange juice

8 cups torn spinach or mixed greens

2 cups sliced strawberries and/or blueberries

¼ cup pecan halves

Snap off and discard woody bases from asparagus. If desired, scrape off scales. Cut asparagus into 1-inch pieces. Cook asparagus, covered, in a small amount of boiling water for 4 to 8 minutes or until crisp-tender; drain. Rinse with cold water. Let asparagus stand in cold water until cool; drain again.

Meanwhile, for dressing, stir together poppy seed or Italian salad dressing, orange peel, and orange juice. Set dressing aside.

In a large salad bowl combine spinach or mixed greens, strawberries or blueberries, and asparagus. Divide salad mixture among four salad plates. Stir dressing again. Drizzle dressing over each salad. Sprinkle with pecans.

Makes 4 servings.

Nutrition information per serving: 232 calories, 4 g protein, 14 g carbohydrate, 19 g fat (2 g saturated), 0 mg cholesterol, 321 mg sodium.

Potato Salad Olé

Potato salad takes a south-of-the-border departure in flavor with the addition of taco seasoning mix, corn, and red kidney beans.

3   medium potatoes (1 pound), halved lengthwise
¾   cup mayonnaise or salad dressing
1   tablespoon taco seasoning mix
1   8-ounce can red kidney beans, rinsed and drained
1   8¾-ounce can whole kernel corn, drained
½   cup chopped green pepper
½   cup sliced celery
¼   cup sliced pitted ripe olives
    Romaine leaves or cabbage leaves
1   small tomato, cut into wedges

In a covered large saucepan cook potatoes in boiling water for 15 to 20 minutes or until just tender; drain well. Cool slightly. Cut potatoes into ¼-inch-thick slices.

Meanwhile, for dressing, in a small mixing bowl combine mayonnaise or salad dressing and taco seasoning mix.

In a large mixing bowl combine kidney beans, corn, chopped green pepper, celery, and olives. Pour dressing over bean mixture. Toss lightly to coat. Add potatoes. Toss lightly again to mix. Cover; chill for 6 to 24 hours.

Serve on romaine- or cabbage-lined salad plates or in a salad bowl. Garnish with tomato wedges.

Makes 6 servings.

Nutrition information per serving: 332 calories, 6 g protein, 29 g carbohydrate, 24 g fat (3 g saturated), 16 mg cholesterol, 429 mg sodium.

Lemon-Basil
Pasta with
Vegetables

Most grocery stores stock several combinations of loose-pack frozen vegetables. Choose the one that strikes your fancy.

1 cup packaged dried orecchiette, medium shell macaroni, corkscrew macaroni, or bow ties

1½ cups loose-pack frozen mixed broccoli, French-style green beans, onions, and red sweet pepper or other vegetable combination

3 tablespoons margarine or butter

1 tablespoon snipped parsley

1 clove garlic, minced

1 teaspoon finely shredded lemon peel

½ teaspoon dried basil, crushed

⅛ teaspoon salt

Dash ground red pepper

Cook pasta according to package directions, adding the frozen vegetables the last 5 minutes of cooking time. Drain pasta and vegetable mixture.

Meanwhile, in a small saucepan melt the margarine or butter. Stir in parsley, garlic, lemon peel, basil, salt, and ground red pepper. Pour over pasta mixture. Toss to coat.

Makes 4 servings.

Nutrition information per serving: 178 calories, 4 g protein, 20 g carbohydrate, 9 g fat (2 g saturated), 0 mg cholesterol, 176 mg sodium.

Fusilli with Pesto

This recipe makes enough pesto for three meals. Chill or freeze the remaining pesto.

For pesto, in a blender container or food processor bowl combine basil, parsley, Parmesan or Romano cheese, oil, nuts, garlic, and salt. Cover and blend or process with several on-off turns until a paste forms, stopping the machine several times and scraping the sides.

To serve, cook pasta according to package directions. Drain. Add about one-third of the pesto to the pasta; toss to coat. If desired, sprinkle with Parmesan cheese.

Store remaining pesto in airtight containers. Chill up to 2 days or freeze up to 1 month. Bring pesto to room temperature before tossing with pasta.

Makes 4 servings.

1 cup firmly packed fresh basil leaves
½ cup firmly packed parsley sprigs with stems removed
½ cup grated Parmesan or Romano cheese
¼ cup olive oil or cooking oil
¼ cup pine nuts, walnuts, or almonds
1 large clove garlic, sliced
¼ teaspoon salt
4 ounces packaged dried fusilli, spaghetti, or other pasta
Finely shredded or grated Parmesan cheese (optional)

Nutrition information per serving: 190 calories, 7 g protein, 24 g carbohydrate, 8 g fat (2 g saturated), 3 mg cholesterol, 124 mg sodium.

In a large saucepan bring 2 quarts water to boiling. Add pasta and, if desired, ½ teaspoon salt. Return to boiling; cook for 5 minutes. Add frozen vegetables. Return to boiling; cook for 5 to 7 minutes more or until pasta is tender but slightly firm and vegetables are crisp-tender. Drain pasta and vegetables.

Meanwhile, for sauce, in a small saucepan melt margarine or butter. Stir in flour, ⅛ teaspoon salt, and pepper. Add milk all at once. Cook and stir until thickened and bubbly. Cook and stir for 1 minute more. Remove from heat. Stir in ½ cup blue cheese and the sour cream.

Pour sauce over pasta mixture. Toss to coat. If desired, sprinkle with additional blue cheese.

Makes 6 servings.

1   **cup packaged dried cut ziti or corkscrew macaroni**
½   **teaspoon salt (optional)**
3   **cups loose-pack frozen broccoli, cauliflower, and carrots**
2   **tablespoons margarine or butter**
2   **tablespoons all-purpose flour**
⅛   **teaspoon salt**
⅛   **teaspoon pepper**
1   **cup milk**
½   **cup crumbled blue cheese (2 ounces)**
⅓   **cup dairy sour cream**
     Crumbled blue cheese (optional)

Nutrition information per serving: 223 calories, 8 g protein, 26 g carbohydrate, 10 g fat (5 g saturated), 16 mg cholesterol, 280 mg sodium.

Ziti with Blue Cheese Sauce

Pass the Bread

Grease twelve 2½-inch muffin cups or line with paper bake cups. Set muffin cups aside.

In a medium mixing bowl stir together flour, ½ cup sugar, wheat germ, baking powder, salt, and baking soda. Make a well in the center of dry mixture.

In another medium mixing bowl combine the eggs, oil, and bananas. Add all at once to the dry mixture. Stir just until moistened (batter should be lumpy). Fold in almonds.

Spoon batter into the prepared muffin cups, filling each ⅔ full. For topping, combine 1 tablespoon sugar and cinnamon. Sprinkle over batter. Bake in a 400° oven about 20 minutes or until golden. Cool in muffin cups on a wire rack for 5 minutes. Remove muffins from muffin cups. Serve warm.

Makes 12 muffins.

1½ **cups all-purpose flour**
½ **cup sugar**
3 **tablespoons toasted wheat germ**
1½ **teaspoons baking powder**
½ **teaspoon salt**
¼ **teaspoon baking soda**
2 **beaten eggs**
½ **cup cooking oil**
3 **ripe medium bananas, mashed (1 cup)**
½ **cup toasted chopped almonds**
1 **tablespoon sugar**
¼ **teaspoon ground cinnamon**

Nutrition information per muffin: 240 calories, 5 g protein, 29 g carbohydrate, 13 g fat (2 g saturated), 36 mg cholesterol, 172 mg sodium.

Banana Almond Muffins

Grease six 1-cup muffin cups. Set muffin cups aside.

In a medium mixing bowl stir together flour, sugar, baking powder, and salt. Make a well in the center of dry mixture.

In another medium mixing bowl combine eggs; milk; margarine, butter, or oil; and orange peel. Add all at once to the dry mixture. Stir just until moistened (batter should be lumpy). Fold in blueberries.

Spoon batter into prepared muffin cups, filling each almost full. If desired, sprinkle tops with coarse sugar. Bake in a 350° oven about 35 minutes or until golden. Cool in muffin cups on a wire rack for 5 minutes. Remove muffins from muffin cups. Serve warm.

Makes 6 large muffins.

If you prefer a dozen smaller muffins, spoon the batter into twelve 2½-inch muffin pan cups and bake in a 375° oven for 20 minutes or until golden.

  2 **cups all-purpose flour**
 ¾ **cup sugar**
2½ **teaspoons baking powder**
 ½ **teaspoon salt**
  2 **beaten eggs**
 ¾ **cup milk**
 ½ **cup melted butter or margarine or cooking oil**
  1 **tablespoon finely shredded orange peel**
  1 **cup fresh or frozen blueberries, thawed**
     Coarse sugar (optional)

Nutrition information per muffin: 425 calories, 7 g protein, 60 g carbohydrate, 18 g fat (10 g saturated), 114 mg cholesterol, 522 mg sodium.

Giant Blueberry Muffins

Marjoram
Muffins

Savory muffins like these complement most main dishes from soups to salads. Serve warm with creamy butter.

Grease twelve 2½-inch muffin cups or line with paper bake cups. Set muffin cups aside.

In a medium mixing bowl stir together flour, sugar, baking powder, marjoram, rosemary, and salt. Make a well in the center of the dry mixture.

In another medium mixing bowl combine egg, milk, and oil. Add all at once to the dry mixture. Stir just until moistened (batter should be lumpy).

Spoon batter into the prepared muffin cups, filling each ⅔ full. Bake in a 400° oven for 20 to 25 minutes or until golden. Cool in muffin cups on a wire rack for 5 minutes. Remove muffins from muffin cups. Serve warm.

Makes 12 muffins.

1¾ **cup all-purpose flour**
¼ **cup sugar**
2 **teaspoons baking powder**
2 **teaspoons snipped fresh marjoram or**
  ½ **teaspoon dried marjoram, crushed**
1 **teaspoon snipped fresh rosemary or**
  ¼ **teaspoon dried rosemary, crushed**
¼ **teaspoon salt**
1 **beaten egg**
¾ **cup milk**
¼ **cup cooking oil**

Nutrition information per muffin: 132 calories, 3 g protein, 18 g carbohydrate, 5 g fat (1 g saturated), 19 mg cholesterol, 118 mg sodium.

Skillet Pepper Corn Bread

If you like, omit the chili pepper and substitute Monterey Jack cheese with peppers for the cheddar cheese. You will save the step of chopping the fresh pepper.

Spray an 8- or 9-inch cast-iron or oven-safe skillet with nonstick coating. Heat skillet in a 400° oven for 5 minutes just before filling.

In a large mixing bowl stir together cornmeal, flour, baking powder, and salt. Make a well in the center of dry mixture.

In a medium mixing bowl beat together eggs, milk, cream-style corn, and oil. Add egg mixture all at once to dry mixture. Stir just until moistened (batter should be lumpy). Fold in cheese and jalapeño pepper.

Pour batter into hot skillet. Bake for 20 to 25 minutes or until a wooden toothpick inserted near center comes out clean. Cool in skillet on wire rack 10 minutes. Serve warm.

Makes 1 loaf (8 servings).

Nonstick spray coating
1 cup cornmeal
½ cup all-purpose flour
2 teaspoons baking powder
¼ teaspoon salt
2 beaten eggs
½ cup milk
1 8¾-ounce can cream-style corn
2 tablespoons cooking oil
½ cup shredded cheddar cheese
1 fresh red or green jalapeño pepper, seeded and finely chopped

Nutrition information per serving: 198 calories, 7 g protein, 26 g carbohydrate, 8 g fat (3 g saturated), 62 mg cholesterol, 317 mg sodium.

Carrot-Zucchini Loaves

The carrots and zucchini add a confettilike look to these moist loaves. Perfect served plain, or spread slices with a thin layer of whipped cream cheese.

Grease bottom and ½ inch up sides of two 8×4×2-inch loaf pans. Set aside.

In a large mixing bowl stir together flour, wheat germ, baking powder, baking soda, and salt. Make a well in the center of dry mixture.

In a medium mixing bowl combine eggs, granulated sugar, zucchini, carrot, brown sugar, and oil and mix well. Add all at once to dry mixture. Stir just until moistened (batter should be lumpy).

Pour batter into loaf pans. Bake in a 350° oven for 45 to 55 minutes or until a wooden toothpick inserted near center comes out clean. (If necessary, cover loosely with foil during last 10 to 15 minutes of baking to prevent overbrowning.) Cool in pans on wire racks 10 minutes. Remove from pans and cool thoroughly on wire racks. Wrap and store overnight before slicing.

Makes 2 loaves (24 servings).

2½	cups all-purpose flour
½	cup toasted wheat germ
2	teaspoons baking powder
½	teaspoon baking soda
½	teaspoon salt
3	beaten eggs
1	cup granulated sugar
1	cup finely shredded zucchini
1	cup finely shredded carrot
½	cup packed brown sugar
½	cup cooking oil

Nutrition information per serving: 151 calories, 3 g protein, 23 g carbohydrate, 6 g fat (1 g saturated), 27 mg cholesterol, 112 mg sodium.

Maple Pumpkin Bread

You can substitute 2 teaspoons pumpkin pie spice for the spices in this fragrant, moist tea bread. Delicious served for an afternoon tea or with coffee for a quick breakfast.

2 cups all-purpose flour

2 teaspoons baking powder

1 teaspoon ground cinnamon

½ teaspoon baking soda

½ teaspoon ground nutmeg

½ teaspoon ground allspice

2 beaten eggs

1 cup packed brown sugar

1 cup canned pumpkin

½ cup maple syrup

⅓ cup cooking oil

1 cup chopped pecans
  Maple Glaze

Grease bottom and ½ inch up sides of a 9×5×3-inch loaf pan. Set pan aside.

In a large mixing bowl stir together flour, baking powder, cinnamon, baking soda, nutmeg, and allspice. Make a well in the center of dry mixture.

In a medium mixing bowl combine eggs, brown sugar, pumpkin, maple syrup, and oil and mix well. Add all at once to dry mixture. Stir just until moistened (batter should be lumpy). Fold in pecans.

Pour batter into loaf pan. Bake in a 350° oven for 60 to 65 minutes or until a wooden toothpick inserted near center comes out clean. (If necessary, cover with foil the last 10 to 15 minutes of baking to prevent overbrowning.) Cool in pan on a wire rack 10 minutes. Remove from pan and cool thoroughly on wire rack. Wrap and store overnight before slicing. Drizzle with Maple Glaze at least 1 hour before serving.

Makes 1 loaf (16 servings).

Maple Glaze: In a small mixing bowl combine ½ cup sifted powdered sugar and 2 tablespoons maple syrup. If necessary, add milk, 1 teaspoon at a time, to make drizzling consistency.

Nutrition information per serving: 238 calories, 3 g protein, 36 g carbohydrate, 10 g fat (1 g saturated), 27 mg cholesterol, 98 mg sodium.

In a medium mixing bowl stir together whole wheat flour, all-purpose flour, baking powder, baking soda, and salt. Using a pastry blender, cut in butter or margarine until mixture resembles coarse crumbs. Make a well in center of dry mixture. Add 1 egg; the buttermilk; brown sugar; and cherries, cranberries, or raisins all at once. Using a fork, stir just until moistened.

Turn dough out onto a lightly floured surface. Quickly knead dough by folding and pressing dough gently for 10 to 12 strokes or until dough is nearly smooth. Shape dough into a 6-inch round loaf. Cut a 4-inch cross, ½ inch deep, on the top.

Place loaf on a greased baking sheet. Brush with remaining egg. Bake in a 375° oven about 35 minutes or until golden. Remove from baking sheet and serve warm.

Makes 1 loaf (8 servings).

1   cup whole wheat flour
1   cup all-purpose flour
1   teaspoon baking powder
½   teaspoon baking soda
¼   teaspoon salt
3   tablespoons butter or margarine
1   beaten egg
¾   cup buttermilk
2   tablespoons brown sugar
⅓   cup dried cherries, dried cranberries,
     or raisins
1   beaten egg

Nutrition information per serving: 196 calories, 6 g protein, 30 g carbohydrate, 6 g fat (3 g saturated), 66 mg cholesterol, 276 mg sodium.

Irish Soda Bread

In a medium mixing bowl stir together flour, baking powder, salt, and baking soda. Using a pastry blender, cut in shortening until mixture resembles coarse crumbs. Make a well in center of dry mixture, then add buttermilk all at once. Using a fork, stir just until moistened.

Turn dough out onto a lightly floured surface. Quickly knead dough by folding and pressing dough gently for 10 to 12 strokes or until dough is nearly smooth. Roll dough into 13-inch circle. Brush with melted butter or margarine. Sprinkle with 1/3 cup Parmesan cheese and the parsley. Cut into 12 wedges. Roll up each wedge from the wide end to the point.

Place crescents, seam side down, about 2 inches apart on an ungreased baking sheet, curving to form crescents. Brush with milk and sprinkle with additional Parmesan cheese. Bake in a 425° oven for 15 to 20 minutes or until golden. Remove crescents from baking sheet and serve warm.

Makes 12 crescents.

2¼ cups all-purpose flour
2 teaspoons baking powder
½ teaspoon salt
¼ teaspoon baking soda
½ cup shortening
¾ cup buttermilk
1 tablespoon butter or margarine, melted
⅓ cup grated Parmesan cheese
2 tablespoons finely snipped fresh parsley
Milk
Grated Parmesan cheese

Nutrition information per crescent: 185 calories, 4 g protein, 18 g carbohydrate, 11 g fat (3 g saturated), 6 mg cholesterol, 264 mg sodium.

Parmesan Cheese Crescents

Cloverleaf Rye Rolls

To make these rolls ahead, wrap the cooled, baked rolls in a single layer of heavy foil. Seal, label, and freeze up to 2 months. To reheat, place baked wrapped rolls in a 350° oven 30 to 35 minutes.

3½ to 4 cups all-purpose flour
2 packages active dry yeast
¼ cup sugar
1 teaspoon salt
2 cups water
2 tablespoons shortening
2 cups rye flour

In a large bowl mix 2¾ cups of the all-purpose flour, the yeast, sugar, and salt. In a medium saucepan heat and stir water and shortening just until warm (120° to 130°) and shortening almost melts. Add shortening mixture to flour mixture. Beat with an electric mixer 30 seconds, scraping sides of bowl constantly. Beat on high speed 3 minutes. Using a wooden spoon, stir in rye flour and as much of the remaining all-purpose flour as you can.

Turn dough out onto a floured surface. Knead in enough of the remaining flour to make a moderately soft dough that is smooth and elastic (6 to 8 minutes total). Shape dough into a ball; place in a lightly greased bowl, turning once to grease surface of dough. Cover; let rise in a warm place until double (about 1 hour). Punch dough down. Turn dough out onto a lightly floured surface. Divide dough in half. Cover; let rest for 10 minutes. Meanwhile, lightly grease twenty-four 2½-inch muffin cups.

Divide each portion of dough into 36 pieces. Shape each piece into a ball, pulling edges under to make a smooth top. Place 3 balls in each muffin cup, smooth side up. Cover and let rise in a warm place until nearly double (about 30 minutes). Bake in a 375° oven 15 to 18 minutes or until golden. Remove from pans. Cool or serve warm.

Makes 24 rolls.

Nutrition information per roll: 110 calories, 3 g protein, 22 g carbohydrate, 1 g fat (0 g saturated), 0 mg cholesterol, 90 mg sodium.

Sweet Dreams

Grease and lightly flour two 9×1½-inch round baking pans. Set aside.

In a large mixing bowl combine flour, sugar, baking soda, cinnamon, baking powder, and salt. Add shredded carrots, pineapple, chopped walnuts, eggs, coconut, buttermilk or sour milk, cooking oil, and vanilla. Stir until combined. Pour batter in prepared pans.

Bake in a 350° oven for 40 to 45 minutes or until tops spring back when touched lightly. Immediately pour Buttermilk Glaze evenly over cakes in pans. Cool in pans on wire racks for 15 minutes. Remove from pans; cool completely on wire racks. Fill and frost with Nutty Cream Cheese Frosting. Top with walnut halves, if desired. Store in the refrigerator.

Makes 16 servings.

Buttermilk Glaze: In a medium saucepan mix ½ cup granulated sugar, ¼ cup buttermilk or sour milk,* ¼ cup margarine or butter, and 2 teaspoons light corn syrup. Bring to boiling; reduce heat. Cook and stir 4 minutes. Remove from heat; stir in ½ teaspoon vanilla.

Nutty Cream Cheese Frosting: In a large bowl beat two 3-ounce packages cream cheese, ½ cup softened margarine or butter, and 2 teaspoons vanilla with an electric mixer on medium to high speed until light and fluffy. Gradually add 4½ to 4¾ cups sifted powdered sugar, beating to spreading consistency. Stir in ½ cup chopped walnuts.

*Note: For sour milk, place 1½ teaspoons lemon juice or vinegar in a measuring cup. Add enough milk to equal ½ cup.

Time to indulge! This deluxe version of carrot cake is topped with not one, but two different icings—a buttermilk glaze and a cream cheese-walnut frosting.

2 cups all-purpose flour
2 cups granulated sugar
2 teaspoons baking soda
1½ teaspoons ground cinnamon
1 teaspoon baking powder
¼ teaspoon salt
4 medium carrots, shredded (2 cups)
1 8¼-ounce can crushed pineapple, drained
1 cup chopped walnuts
3 eggs
½ cup coconut
¼ cup buttermilk or sour milk*
¼ cup cooking oil
1 teaspoon vanilla
   Buttermilk Glaze
   Nutty Cream Cheese Frosting
16 walnut halves (optional)

Nutrition information per serving: 728 calories, 8 g protein, 105 g carbohydrate, 33 g fat (8 g saturated), 69 mg cholesterol, 466 mg sodium.

Buttermilk Carrot Cake

Sponge Cake with Broiled Macadamia-Coconut Topping

Hot milk sponge cake crowned with an extra-easy broiled topping—so delicious everyone will want seconds!

1 cup all-purpose flour
1 teaspoon baking powder
2 eggs
½ teaspoon vanilla
1 cup granulated sugar
½ cup milk
2 tablespoons margarine or butter
Broiled Macadamia-Coconut Topping

Grease a 9×9×2-inch baking pan. Combine flour and baking powder. Set aside.

In a large mixing bowl beat eggs and vanilla with an electric mixer on high speed about 4 minutes or until thick and lemon-colored. Gradually add sugar, beating on medium speed about 5 minutes or until sugar is almost dissolved. Gradually add the flour mixture, beating on low to medium speed just until combined. In a small saucepan heat milk and margarine or butter until the margarine melts. Add milk mixture to egg mixture, stirring just until combined. Pour batter into prepared pan.

Bake in a 350° oven for 25 to 30 minutes or until top springs back when lightly touched. Cool in pan on wire rack for 10 minutes. Carefully spread Broiled Macadamia-Coconut Topping over warm cake. Broil about 4 inches from the heat for 2 to 3 minutes or until lightly browned and bubbly. Cool completely in pan on wire rack.

Makes 9 servings.

Broiled Macadamia-Coconut Topping: In a small mixing bowl stir together ½ cup flaked coconut, ¼ cup packed brown sugar, ¼ cup chopped macadamia nuts or slivered almonds, 2 tablespoons margarine or butter, and 1 tablespoon milk.

Nutrition information per serving: 271 calories, 4 g protein, 41 g carbohydrate, 11 g fat (3 g saturated), 48 mg cholesterol, 87 mg sodium.

Chocolate Fudge Cake

Sour cream makes this chocolate cake moist and tender. Pipe a decorative border, add a special greeting, and top with some candles for the ultimate birthday cake.

Grease and lightly flour two 8×1½-inch or 9×1½-inch round baking pans. Combine flour, baking soda, and salt. Set aside.

In a large mixing bowl beat shortening with an electric mixer on medium to high speed about 30 seconds or until softened. Add sugar and vanilla; beat until combined. Add eggs, one at a time, beating well after each addition. Beat in cooled chocolate and sour cream. Alternately add flour mixture and cold water, beating on low to medium speed after each addition just until combined. Pour batter into prepared pans.

Bake in a 350° oven for 25 to 30 minutes or until a wooden toothpick inserted in centers comes out clean. Cool in pans on wire racks 10 minutes. Remove from pans. Cool completely on wire racks. Fill and frost cake with Sour Cream-Fudge Frosting. Store in refrigerator.

Makes 12 servings.

Sour Cream-Fudge Frosting: In a medium saucepan melt 3 ounces unsweetened chocolate and ⅓ cup margarine or butter over low heat. Remove from heat; cool. Stir in ½ cup dairy sour cream and 1 teaspoon vanilla. Gradually add 3 cups sifted powdered sugar, beating until smooth and of spreading consistency.

Nutrition information per serving: 500 calories, 5 g protein, 68 g carbohydrate, 26 g fat (9 g saturated), 44 mg cholesterol, 276 mg sodium.

1¾ cups all-purpose flour
1 teaspoon baking soda
½ teaspoon salt
½ cup shortening
1½ cups granulated sugar
½ teaspoon vanilla
2 eggs
3 ounces unsweetened chocolate, melted and cooled
½ cup dairy sour cream
1 cup cold water
Sour Cream-Fudge Frosting

Lemon Crystal Cupcakes

A mixture of fresh lemon juice and sugar gives these little gems a crystally coating.

2	**cups all-purpose flour**
2½	**teaspoons baking powder**
¼	**teaspoon salt**
⅔	**cup shortening**
1	**cup granulated sugar**
3	**eggs**
⅔	**cup milk**
1	**tablespoon finely shredded lemon peel**
⅔	**cup granulated sugar**
⅓	**cup lemon juice**
	Crystal sugar (optional)
	Violets (optional)

Grease and lightly flour twenty 2½-inch muffin cups. Stir together flour, baking powder, and salt.

In a large mixing bowl beat shortening with an electric mixer on medium to high speed for 30 seconds or until softened. Add 1 cup sugar; beat until combined. Add eggs, one at a time, beating well after each addition. Alternately add flour mixture and milk, beating on low to medium speed after each addition just until combined. Stir in lemon peel. Pour batter into prepared muffin cups. Fill any remaining muffin cups with water to avoid damaging pan.

Bake in a 350° oven for 20 to 25 minutes or until a wooden toothpick inserted in centers comes out clean. Cool in pans on wire racks for 5 minutes. Remove from pans. Place cupcakes upside-down on wire racks set over waxed paper.

In a small mixing bowl stir together ⅔ cup sugar and lemon juice. Brush sugar mixture over warm cupcakes until all is absorbed. Cool completely. Sprinkle with crystal sugar and top with violets, if desired.

Makes 20 cupcakes.

Nutrition information per cupcake: 184 calories, 2 g protein, 26 g carbohydrate, 8 g fat (2 g saturated), 33 mg cholesterol, 86 mg sodium.

Grease a 13×9×2-inch baking pan. Combine flour, baking powder, cinnamon, nutmeg, salt, cloves, and baking soda. Set aside.

In a large mixing bowl beat margarine or butter with an electric mixer on medium to high speed about 30 seconds or until softened. Add sugar; beat until combined. Add eggs, one at a time, beating well after each addition. Alternately add flour mixture and applesauce, beating on low to medium speed after each addition just until combined. Stir in raisins and walnuts. Pour batter into the prepared pan.

Bake in a 350° oven for 35 to 40 minutes or until a wooden toothpick inserted in center comes out clean. Cool completely in pan on a wire rack. Frost with Browned Butter Frosting.

Makes 12 servings.

Browned Butter Frosting: In a small saucepan heat ½ cup margarine or butter over low heat until melted; continue heating until margarine or butter turns a delicate brown. Remove from heat; pour into small mixing bowl. Add 4 cups sifted powdered sugar, 2 tablespoons milk, and 1 teaspoon vanilla; beat with an electric mixer on low speed until combined. Beat on medium to high speed, adding additional milk, if necessary, to make frosting of a spreading consistency.

After icing the cake, pull the tines of a fork through the top of the frosting to create a lattice pattern as shown in the photograph.

2½ cups all-purpose flour
1½ teaspoons baking powder
1 teaspoon ground cinnamon
¾ teaspoon ground nutmeg
½ teaspoon salt
½ teaspoon ground cloves
¼ teaspoon baking soda
½ cup margarine or butter
2 cups granulated sugar
2 eggs
1½ cups applesauce
½ cup raisins
½ cup chopped walnuts
Browned Butter Frosting

Nutrition information per serving: 572 calories, 5 g protein, 98 g carbohydrate, 20 g fat (4 g saturated), 36 mg cholesterol, 354 mg sodium.

Applesauce Cake with Browned Butter Frosting

Grease and lightly flour a 15×10×1-inch jelly-roll pan. Stir together flour, baking powder, salt, and apple pie spice. Set aside.

Drain apricots, reserving ⅓ cup syrup. Finely chop apricots. In a small saucepan combine chopped apricots, reserved apricot syrup, and 2 tablespoons sugar. Bring apricot mixture to boiling; reduce heat to low. Cook, stirring and mashing with a spoon, about 4 minutes or until thickened. Remove from heat; cool to room temperature. Set aside.

In a large mixing bowl beat eggs with an electric mixer on high speed about 5 minutes or until thick and lemon-colored. Gradually add apricot mixture and ½ cup sugar, beating on medium speed until sugar is almost dissolved. Sprinkle flour mixture over egg mixture; fold in gently, just until combined. Spread batter evenly in prepared pan. Sprinkle with nuts.

Bake in a 375° oven for 12 to 15 minutes or until top springs back when lightly touched. Immediately loosen edges of cake; turn out onto a towel sprinkled with powdered sugar. Starting with a narrow end, roll up warm cake and towel together. Cool on a wire rack. Unroll cake. Spread Cream Cheese Filling on cake to within 1 inch of edges. Reroll cake without towel. Chill for 2 to 24 hours.

Makes 10 servings.

Cream Cheese Filling: In a small mixing bowl combine two 3-ounce packages cream cheese, softened; ¼ cup margarine or butter, softened; and ½ teaspoon vanilla. Beat with an electric mixer on medium to high speed until fluffy. Beat in 1½ cups sifted powdered sugar and 1 tablespoon milk.

Once you spread the batter in the pan, sprinkle it with nuts to create this stunning nut-covered dessert roll.

1   cup all-purpose flour
1   teaspoon baking powder
¼   teaspoon salt
½   teaspoon apple pie spice
1   8¾-ounce can unpeeled apricot halves
      (in syrup)
2   tablespoons granulated sugar
3   eggs
½   cup granulated sugar
¾   cup finely chopped hazelnuts or pecans
      Sifted powdered sugar
      Cream Cheese Filling

Nutrition information per serving: 351 calories, 6 g protein, 45 g carbohydrate, 18 g fat (6 g saturated), 83 mg cholesterol, 217 mg sodium.

Apricot-Hazelnut Cake Roll

Vanilla-Fudge Marble Cake

Although not a true pound cake, this two-toned ring looks and tastes the part. Serve it with ice cream for a sure-to-please dessert.

2¾ cups sifted all-purpose flour
1½ teaspoons baking powder
½ teaspoon baking soda
½ teaspoon salt
¾ cup margarine or butter
1½ cups granulated sugar
2 teaspoons vanilla
2 eggs
1¼ cups buttermilk or sour milk
⅔ cup chocolate-flavored syrup
Semisweet Chocolate Icing

Grease and lightly flour a 10-inch fluted tube pan. Mix flour, baking powder, baking soda, and salt. Set aside.

In a large bowl beat margarine on low to medium speed with an electric mixer about 30 seconds. Add sugar and vanilla; beat until fluffy. Add eggs, one at a time, beating on low to medium speed 1 minute after each addition and scraping bowl frequently. Add flour mixture and buttermilk alternately to beaten mixture, beating on low speed after each addition just until combined. Reserve 2 cups batter. Spoon remaining batter into prepared pan.

In a small bowl mix chocolate-flavored syrup and reserved batter. Beat on low speed until well combined. Pour chocolate batter over vanilla batter in pan. Do not mix.

Bake in a 350° oven about 50 minutes or until a wooden toothpick inserted near center comes out clean. Cool 15 minutes on rack. Remove from pan; cool completely on wire rack. Drizzle cake with Semisweet Chocolate Icing.

Makes 12 servings.

Semisweet Chocolate Icing: In small saucepan heat ½ cup semisweet chocolate pieces, 2 tablespoons margarine or butter, 1 tablespoon light corn syrup, and ¼ teaspoon vanilla over low heat, stirring until chocolate melts and mixture is smooth. Use immediately.

Nutrition information per serving: 412 calories, 5 g protein, 63 g carbohydrate, 17 g fat (3 g saturated), 36 mg cholesterol, 391 mg sodium.

Strawberry-Mascarpone Dessert Pizza

Mascarpone cheese looks and tastes like cream cheese except it's richer. Look for it at supermarkets, cheese shops, and Italian specialty stores.

For crust, in a medium mixing bowl combine flour and brown sugar. Cut in margarine or butter until mixture resembles coarse crumbs. Press firmly into an 11- to 13-inch pizza pan. Bake in a 400° oven 10 to 15 minutes or until light brown. Cool completely.

Just before serving, in a medium mixing bowl beat whipping cream with an electric mixer on low speed just until soft peaks form. Add mascarpone cheese or cream cheese, powdered sugar, and lemon peel; beat until fluffy (mixture will thicken as it is beaten).

Spread cheese mixture atop cooled crust. Top with strawberries. Garnish with chocolate curls or grated chocolate, if desired. Serve immediately.

Makes 12 servings.

1⅓ cups all-purpose flour
⅓ cup packed brown sugar
⅔ cup margarine or butter, softened
⅔ cup whipping cream
8 ounces mascarpone cheese or soft-style cream cheese
¾ cup sifted powdered sugar
½ teaspoon finely shredded lemon peel
4 cups sliced strawberries
Chocolate curls or grated chocolate (optional)

Nutrition information per serving: 329 calories, 6 g protein, 27 g carbohydrate, 24 g fat (10 g saturated), 42 mg cholesterol, 138 mg sodium.

In a large mixing bowl combine brownie mix, water, oil, and egg. Stir until well combined. Spread dough evenly into a greased 12-inch pizza pan with ½-inch sides. Bake in a 375° oven for 18 to 20 minutes. Cool completely.

Cut crust into 12 wedges; do not remove from pan. Place small scoops of chocolate ice cream on each wedge. Cover tightly and freeze until firm.

Just before serving, pour warm White Chocolate Sauce over ice cream. Sprinkle with cut-up candy bars. If desired, sprinkle with chopped nuts and garnish with fresh strawberries. Serve immediately.

Makes 12 servings.

White Chocolate Sauce: In a heavy medium saucepan bring ⅔ cup whipping cream and 1 teaspoon vanilla just to boiling, stirring frequently. Remove saucepan from heat. In a small mixing bowl beat 1 egg yolk, ⅓ cup sugar, and 2 to 4 tablespoons of the hot whipping cream mixture with an electric mixer on medium speed for 2 to 3 minutes or until thick and lemon-colored. Gradually stir about half of the remaining whipping cream mixture into the egg yolk mixture. Return all to the saucepan. Cook and stir over medium heat just until mixture returns to boiling. Remove from heat. Stir in 2 ounces (½ cup) grated white baking bar. Continue stirring until bar melts. Cover the surface with plastic wrap and cool for 15 minutes. Stir before serving. Store any remaining sauce in the refrigerator.

Try strawberry, coffee, or your personal favorite flavor of ice cream on these decadent brownie pizza wedges.

1	**21½-ounce package fudge brownie mix**
½	**cup water**
¼	**cup cooking oil**
1	**egg**
1	**quart chocolate ice cream**
	White Chocolate Sauce
2	**cups cut-up candy bars (chocolate-coated caramel-topped nougat bars, chocolate-covered English toffee, chocolate-covered peanut butter cups, and/or white chocolate candy bars)**
¼	**cup chopped nuts (optional)**
	Sliced fresh strawberries (optional)

Nutrition information per serving: 483 calories, 5 g protein, 72 g carbohydrate, 21 g fat (10 g saturated), 62 mg cholesterol, 259 mg sodium.

Candy-Bar Pizza Sundaes

For filling, in a medium saucepan combine sugar, flour, and salt. Stir in milk. Cook and stir over medium heat until thickened and bubbly. Reduce heat; cook and stir for 2 minutes more. Remove from heat. Stir 1 cup of the hot mixture into eggs. Return to saucepan; cook and stir until thickened. Cook and stir for 2 minutes more. Do not boil. Remove from heat. Stir in butter or margarine, lime peel, and juice. Fold in yogurt. Tint with food coloring. Cover surface of filling with plastic wrap; cool.

On a floured surface roll half of the pastry into a 12-inch circle. Line a 9-inch pie plate with pastry. Trim and flute edge; prick pastry. Bake in a 450° oven for 10 to 12 minutes. Cool.

Divide remaining pastry in half. Roll each half into circles ⅛ inch thick; cut an 8¾-inch circle out of one portion and an 8-inch circle out of other portion. Place circles on a baking sheet; prick pastry. Bake in a 450° oven for 10 minutes. Cool.

Brush the pastry shell with some of the jelly. Place about 1 cup of the filling in pastry shell. Cover with 8-inch pastry round; brush with jelly. Spread with 1¼ cups of filling. Top with the 8¾-inch pastry. Brush with remaining jelly. Top with remaining filling. Cover; chill pie overnight. If desired, garnish with whipped cream, kiwifruit slices, and lime slices just before serving.

Makes 8 servings.

¾ cup sugar

⅓ cup all-purpose flour

⅛ teaspoon salt

1¾ cups milk

3 beaten eggs

¼ cup butter or margarine

2 teaspoons finely shredded lime peel

¼ cup lime juice

1 8-ounce carton lemon yogurt
 Few drops green food coloring
 Pastry for Double-Crust Pie (see recipe, page 311)

¼ cup apple jelly
 Whipped cream (optional)

2 kiwifruit, peeled, halved lengthwise, and sliced (optional)

1 or 2 lime slices (optional)

Nutrition information per serving: 507 calories, 9 g protein, 60 g carbohydrate, 26 g fat (9 g saturated), 100 mg cholesterol, 294 mg sodium.

Kiwi-Lime Pie

Old-Fashioned Apple Pie

Our version of the quintessential American dessert is bursting with apples and perfectly spiced. Serve it warm with cheddar cheese, if desired.

6 cups peeled, thinly sliced tart apples
1 tablespoon lemon juice
½ cup granulated sugar
¼ cup all-purpose flour
¼ cup packed brown sugar
½ teaspoon ground cinnamon
¼ teaspoon ground nutmeg
   Dash ground cloves
   Pastry for Double-Crust Pie
1 tablespoon butter or margarine
   Milk (optional)

In a large mixing bowl toss apples with lemon juice. Combine granulated sugar, flour, brown sugar, cinnamon, nutmeg, and cloves. Toss until apples are coated. Set apple mixture aside.

Prepare Pastry for Double-Crust Pie. Divide dough in half. Form each half into a ball. On a lightly floured surface, roll out 1 ball of dough into a 12-inch circle. Ease pastry into a 9-inch pie plate.

Transfer apple mixture to pastry-lined pie plate. Dot with butter or margarine. Trim pastry even with pie plate. For top crust, roll out remaining dough. Cut slits in top crust. Place top crust on the filling. Seal and flute the edge. Brush with milk, if desired.

To prevent overbrowning, cover the edge of the pie with foil. Bake in a 375° oven for 25 minutes. Remove foil; bake for 20 to 25 minutes more or until the top is golden brown and apples are tender.

Makes 6 to 8 servings.

Pastry for Double-Crust Pie: Stir together 2 cups all-purpose flour and 1 teaspoon salt. Cut in ⅔ cup shortening. Sprinkle 6 to 7 tablespoons cold water, 1 tablespoon at a time, over the flour mixture, tossing gently after each addition until all is moistened. Form dough into a ball.

Nutrition information per serving: 534 calories, 5 g protein, 74 g carbohydrate, 26 g fat (7 g saturated), 5 mg cholesterol, 201 mg sodium.

Plum Dumplings

To make 8 of these plump dumplings, use Pastry for Double-Crust Pie (see recipe, page 311) and double the remaining ingredients.

(see recipe, page 311)

Pastry for Single-Crust Pie
3 **tablespoons brown sugar**
2 **teaspoons butter or margarine**
⅛ **teaspoon ground cloves**
   Dash ground nutmeg
4 **ripe purple plums**
1 **tablespoon milk**
4 **teaspoons granulated sugar**
¼ **teaspoon ground cinnamon**
   Vanilla or cinnamon ice cream (optional)

Prepare pastry. On a lightly floured surface, roll pastry into an 11-inch circle. Cut into four 5½-inch squares. If desired, cut small leaf shapes from any remaining pastry.

In a small mixing bowl stir together brown sugar, butter or margarine, cloves, and nutmeg; set aside.

For each dumpling, cut 1 plum in half and remove pit. Spoon one-fourth of the brown sugar mixture onto 1 plum half; replace remaining half. Place the filled plum on a pastry square. Bring up corners of dough and pinch edges and corners together to seal. Place dumpling in a shallow baking pan. Brush with milk. If desired, decorate dumplings with pastry leaves, pressing firmly to secure. Stir together granulated sugar and cinnamon; sprinkle over dumplings.

Bake in a 375° oven about 35 minutes or until pastry is brown. Serve warm and, if desired, with ice cream.

Makes 4 servings.

Pastry for Single-Crust Pie: Stir together 1¼ cups all-purpose flour and ¼ teaspoon salt. Cut in ⅓ cup shortening. Sprinkle 3 to 4 tablespoons cold water, 1 tablespoon at a time, over the flour mixture, tossing gently after each addition until all is moistened. Form dough into a ball.

Nutrition information per serving: 385 calories, 4 g protein, 49 g carbohydrate, 20 g fat (6 g saturated), 5 mg cholesterol, 158 mg sodium.

Strawberry
Tarts

Serve these dainty tarts on your best china dessert plates lined with paper doilies.

In a mixing bowl beat butter or margarine and cream cheese until well mixed. Stir in flour. Divide dough into 16 pieces. Press into 16 ungreased, 2½-inch muffin pan cups, pressing dough onto the bottom and halfway up sides. Bake in a 400° oven for 12 to 15 minutes or until golden. Cool on wire rack. Remove shells from muffin cups.

For glaze, in a blender container or food processor bowl, combine ¾ cup of the strawberries and the water. Cover and blend or process until smooth. If necessary, add enough additional water to make ¾ cup. In a small saucepan combine sugar and cornstarch. Stir in pureed strawberry mixture. Cook and stir over medium heat until mixture is thickened and bubbly. Cook and stir for 2 minutes more. Stir in orange peel and red food coloring, if desired. Cool for 10 minutes.

In a heavy small saucepan melt chocolate and shortening. Drizzle chocolate mixture into the bottom of the cooled pastry shells. Arrange whole strawberries, stem end down, in tart shells. Cut any large berries in half. Spoon glaze over berries. Chill for 1 to 2 hours. (After 2 hours, filling may begin to water out.) Serve with whipped cream, and garnish with fresh mint, if desired.

Makes 16 tarts.

½ cup butter or margarine, softened
1 3-ounce package cream cheese, softened
1 cup all-purpose flour
3 cups small whole strawberries
⅓ cup water
⅓ cup granulated sugar
1 tablespoon cornstarch
½ teaspoon finely shredded orange peel (optional)
  Several drops red food coloring (optional)
⅓ cup semisweet chocolate pieces
1 teaspoon shortening
  Whipped cream (optional)
  Fresh mint (optional)

Nutrition information per tart: 144 calories, 2 g protein, 5 g carbohydrate, 9 g fat (5 g saturated), 21 mg cholesterol, 83 mg sodium.

In a medium mixing bowl beat the ⅓ cup sugar, butter or margarine, shortening, and the ¼ teaspoon vanilla with an electric mixer on medium speed until combined. Stir in the flour and salt until crumbly. Pat into the bottom of a 9-inch springform pan. Set aside.

Place apple slices in a single layer in a shallow baking pan. Cover with foil. Bake in a 400° oven for 15 minutes.

Meanwhile, for filling, in a large mixing bowl beat the cream cheese, the ½ cup sugar, and the ½ teaspoon vanilla with an electric mixer on medium to high speed until fluffy. Add the eggs all at once, beating on low speed just until combined. Pour into pastry-lined pan. Arrange warm apple slices over filling. Combine the remaining ⅓ cup sugar and cinnamon. Sprinkle filling with sugar mixture and almonds.

Bake in a 375° oven about 35 minutes or until center appears nearly set when shaken. Cool 15 minutes. Loosen crust from sides of pan. Cool 30 minutes more; remove sides of pan. Cover; chill 4 to 24 hours.

Makes 12 servings.

For a change of pace, try this apple-topped cheesecake for a holiday dessert.

⅓ cup sugar

⅓ cup butter or margarine

1 tablespoon shortening

¼ teaspoon vanilla

1 cup all-purpose flour

⅛ teaspoon salt

4 cups peeled, cored, and sliced apples

2 8-ounce packages cream cheese

½ cup granulated sugar

½ teaspoon vanilla

2 eggs

⅓ cup sugar

1 teaspoon ground cinnamon

¼ cup sliced almonds

Nutrition information per serving: 245 calories, 6 g protein, 34 g carbohydrate, 22 g fat (12 g saturated), 91 mg cholesterol, 198 mg sodium.

Bavarian Apple Cheesecake

In a medium mixing bowl stir together the fresh fruit and, if desired, the ¼ cup granulated sugar. Set aside.

For the shortcake, in a medium mixing bowl combine the flour, baking powder, cream of tartar, and baking soda. Cut in the butter or margarine until mixture resembles coarse crumbs. Make a well in the center; add the buttermilk or sour milk, poppy seed, and the 1 teaspoon lemon peel all at once. Stir just until dough clings together.

On a lightly floured surface, knead dough gently for 10 to 12 strokes. Pat dough into an 8-inch circle on a baking sheet. Using a sharp knife, cut into 10 wedges, but do not separate. Bake in a 450° oven for 15 to 18 minutes or until golden.

Meanwhile, in a medium mixing bowl beat the whipping cream with an electric mixer on low speed just until soft peaks form. Add the mascarpone cheese or soft-style cream cheese, the ¾ cup powdered sugar, and the ½ teaspoon lemon peel. Beat until fluffy (the mixture will thicken as it is beaten).

Separate the warm shortcake into wedges. Split wedges. Pipe or spread the mascarpone cheese mixture over the bottom layers of the wedges. Spoon the fresh fruit onto the cheese layer. Add shortcake tops. Serve immediately. Pass any remaining fresh fruit.

Makes 10 servings.

Mascarpone, a soft Italian cheese, and whipping cream make an ultra-rich shortcake filling.

    6 cups cut up, peeled kiwifruit, mangoes, or
        peaches; sliced strawberries; or whole
        raspberries or blueberries
    ¼ cup granulated sugar (optional)
    2 cups all-purpose flour
    1 tablespoon baking powder
    ½ teaspoon cream of tartar
    ¼ teaspoon baking soda
    ½ cup butter or margarine
    ¾ cup buttermilk or sour milk
    2 tablespoons poppy seed
    1 teaspoon finely shredded lemon peel
    ⅔ cup whipping cream
    8 ounces mascarpone cheese or soft-style
        cream cheese
    ¾ cup sifted powdered sugar
    ½ teaspoon finely shredded lemon peel

Nutrition information per serving: 404 calories, 9 g protein, 39 g carbohydrate, 27 g fat (16 g saturated), 76 mg cholesterol, 274 mg sodium.

Lemon-Poppy Seed Shortcake

Poached Pears with White Chocolate Sauce

A rich, creamy white chocolate sauce drizzles down the sides of pears poached in sweet white wine for a company-pleasing dessert.

4 medium pears
1 cup sweet white wine
1 cup water
¼ cup sugar
1 teaspoon vanilla
  White Chocolate Sauce
  Fresh red raspberries (optional)

Peel pears, leaving stems intact. To core pears, use an apple corer or the rounded tip of a vegetable peeler. Push the corer or peeler through the blossom end of each pear, but do not cut through the stem end. Turn corer or peeler to loosen the core. Remove and discard core. Set pears aside.

In a large saucepan bring wine, water, sugar, and vanilla to boiling. Place the pears in the pan, stem ends up; spoon the wine mixture over the pears. Reduce heat. Cover and simmer for 15 to 20 minutes or until the pears are tender. Spoon some of the cooking liquid over the pears. Remove saucepan from heat. Let pears cool in liquid.

To serve, place each pear in a dessert dish. Spoon some of the cooking liquid over each. Drizzle with White Chocolate Sauce. Garnish with fresh raspberries, if desired.

Makes 4 servings.

White Chocolate Sauce: In a small saucepan melt ¼ cup white baking pieces and 1 tablespoon butter or margarine over low heat. Add ⅓ cup sugar. Gradually stir in ½ cup milk. Bring to boiling; reduce heat. Boil gently over low heat for 8 minutes, stirring frequently. Remove from heat. Cool slightly (about 30 minutes).

Nutrition information per serving: 311 calories, 2 g protein, 53 g carbohydrate, 7 g fat (4 g saturated), 10 mg cholesterol, 57 mg sodium.

Thaw frozen cherries and blueberries, if using. Do not drain.

In a 2-quart square baking dish combine cherries and blueberries. Stir in granulated sugar and 3 tablespoons flour.

For topping, in a medium mixing bowl combine brown sugar and ¼ cup flour. Cut in butter or margarine until mixture resembles coarse crumbs. Stir in oats and nuts. Sprinkle topping over cherry mixture.

Bake in a 375° oven about 40 minutes or until filling is bubbly and topping is golden. Serve warm and, if desired, with vanilla or cinnamon ice cream.

Makes 6 servings.

4 cups fresh or frozen pitted tart
   red cherries

1 cup fresh or frozen blueberries

½ cup granulated sugar

3 tablespoons all-purpose flour

½ cup packed brown sugar

¼ cup all-purpose flour

¼ cup butter or margarine

½ cup rolled oats

½ cup chopped pecans or walnuts
   Vanilla or cinnamon ice cream (optional)

Nutrition information per serving: 368 calories, 4 g protein, 60 g carbohydrate, 15 g fat (5 g saturated), 20 mg cholesterol, 87 mg sodium.

Cherry-Berry Crisp

Thaw frozen peach slices, if using. Do not drain. In a Dutch oven stir together the peaches, 1 cup granulated sugar, water, cornstarch, and cinnamon. Cook and stir until mixture is thickened and bubbly. Keep warm.

Meanwhile, for pecan filling, stir together brown sugar and melted butter or margarine. Add pecans; toss to mix. Set aside.

For dough, in a large mixing bowl stir together flour, 2 teaspoons granulated sugar, baking powder, baking soda, and salt. Cut in shortening until mixture resembles coarse crumbs. Make a well in the center; add buttermilk. Stir just until dough clings together.

Turn dough out onto a lightly floured surface. Knead gently for 10 to 12 strokes. Roll dough into a 12×8-inch rectangle; spread with pecan filling. Roll up from one of the long sides. Cut into twelve 1-inch-thick slices.

Transfer hot peach mixture to a shallow 3-quart baking dish. Place slices, cut side down, on top of the hot peach mixture. Bake in a 400° oven for 25 to 30 minutes or until topping is golden. Serve warm with half-and-half or light cream, if desired.

Makes 12 servings.

8 cups sliced, peeled, fresh or frozen peaches
1 cup granulated sugar
1 cup water
2 tablespoons cornstarch
1 teaspoon ground cinnamon
¾ cup packed brown sugar
¼ cup butter or margarine, melted
1½ cups chopped pecans
2 cups all-purpose flour
2 teaspoons granulated sugar
2 teaspoons baking powder
½ teaspoon baking soda
½ teaspoon salt
½ cup shortening
¾ cup buttermilk
Half-and-half or light cream (optional)

Nutrition information per serving: 438 calories, 4 g protein, 60 g carbohydrate, 22 g fat (5 g saturated), 11 mg cholesterol, 261 mg sodium.

Peach-Praline Cobbler

Chocolate and Pear Bread Pudding

Cream cheese and semisweet chocolate pieces make an exceptionally rich custard in this fruity bread pudding.

In a large mixing bowl beat cream cheese, the ⅔ cup sugar, lemon peel, vanilla, the ¼ teaspoon nutmeg, and the ¼ teaspoon cinnamon with an electric mixer on low speed until smooth. Beat in eggs, 1 at a time, beating just until combined after each addition. With a large spoon, stir in milk, half-and-half, or light cream; bread; pears; and chocolate pieces. Pour mixture into an ungreased 2-quart square baking dish, stirring gently to distribute chocolate pieces.

In a small mixing bowl combine the 1 teaspoon sugar, the ⅛ teaspoon nutmeg, and the ⅛ teaspoon cinnamon. Sprinkle over pear mixture. Place dish in a 13×9×2-inch baking pan; set on oven rack. Pour hot water into the 13×9×2-inch baking pan to a depth of 1 inch. Bake in a 350° oven about 45 minutes or until a knife inserted near the center comes out clean. Serve warm or cool.

Makes 9 servings.

1 8-ounce package cream cheese, softened
⅔ cup sugar
1 teaspoon finely shredded lemon peel
1 teaspoon vanilla
¼ teaspoon ground nutmeg
¼ teaspoon ground cinnamon
4 eggs
1½ cups milk, half-and-half, or light cream
3 cups dry bread cubes (about 4 slices bread)
4 medium pears, peeled, cored, and thinly sliced (2 cups)
⅓ cup miniature semisweet chocolate pieces
1 teaspoon sugar
⅛ teaspoon ground nutmeg
⅛ teaspoon ground cinnamon

Nutrition information per serving: 306 calories, 8 g protein, 39 g carbohydrate, 14 g fat (7 g saturated), 126 mg cholesterol, 176 mg sodium.

Tantalizing Nibbles

329

Mini Balls of Fire

Temper these fire-breathing meatballs with a cool chutney for dipping. The heat comes from habanero chili peppers, also called Scotch Bonnet peppers.

In a large mixing bowl stir together egg, bread crumbs, milk, mint or cilantro, chili pepper, salt, cinnamon, ginger, nutmeg, black pepper, and cloves. Add lamb or beef; mix well.

Shape meat mixture into 1-inch meatballs. Place in a 15×10×1-inch baking pan. Bake in a 350° oven for 15 to 20 minutes or until no longer pink. Drain on paper towels. Serve warm with chutney.

Makes 48 meatballs.

1   **beaten egg**
¼   **cup fine dry bread crumbs**
¼   **cup milk**
2   **tablespoons snipped fresh mint or cilantro**
1½   **teaspoons finely chopped habanero chili pepper**
½   **teaspoon salt**
½   **teaspoon ground cinnamon**
½   **teaspoon ground ginger**
¼   **teaspoon ground nutmeg**
¼   **teaspoon ground black pepper**
⅛   **teaspoon ground cloves**
1   **pound ground lamb or beef**
1   **cup chutney**

Nutrition information per meatball: 36 calories, 2 g protein, 4 g carbohydrate, 1 g fat (1 g saturated), 11 mg cholesterol, 35 mg sodium.

In a saucepan cook spinach, shallots or onion, and garlic in one tablespoon boiling water for 3 to 5 minutes or until tender. Drain; press out excess moisture. Stir in salsa.

Thoroughly wash oysters. Open shells with an oyster knife or other blunt-tipped knife. Remove oysters and dry. Discard flat top shells. Wash bottom shells. Place each oyster in a bottom shell.

Spoon spinach-salsa mixture over oysters. Combine bread crumbs and cumin. Toss with melted margarine or butter. Sprinkle over oysters.

Line a shallow baking pan with rock salt to about ½-inch depth. (Or, use crumpled foil to keep shells from tipping over.) Arrange oysters on top. Bake in a 425° oven for 10 to 12 minutes or until edges of oysters begin to curl.

Makes 6 to 8 servings.

Make this spicy version of Oysters Rockefeller as hot as your tongue can take by choosing the salsa you like.

- 2 cups chopped fresh spinach
- ¼ cup chopped shallots or onion
- 2 cloves garlic, minced
- 1 cup salsa
- 24 oysters in shells
- ¼ cup fine dry bread crumbs
- ¼ teaspoon ground cumin
- 1 tablespoon margarine or butter, melted

Nutrition information per serving: 230 calories, 21 g protein, 19 g carbohydrate, 8 g fat (1 g saturated), 0 mg cholesterol, 431 mg sodium.

Oysters Salsafeller

Spicy Chicken Wings

Whew! These wings are really hot but the cool dipping sauce helps tame the flame.

Cut off and discard tips of chicken wings. Cut wing at joints to form 24 pieces. Rinse pieces and pat dry. Fry wing pieces, a few at a time, in deep hot oil (375°) for 8 to 10 minutes or until golden brown and no longer pink. Drain on paper towels. Keep pieces warm in a 300° oven while frying remaining pieces. Transfer wings to a serving dish.

In a saucepan melt margarine or butter. Stir in hot pepper sauce. Pour over wings, turning wings to coat.

For dipping sauce, in a small mixing bowl stir together sour cream, mayonnaise or salad dressing, basil, parsley, and milk. Serve wings with dipping sauce. Garnish sauce with fresh basil, if desired.

Makes 8 to 12 servings.

12 **chicken wings (about 2 pounds)**
    Oil for deep-fat frying
3   **tablespoons margarine or butter**
1   **2-ounce bottle hot pepper sauce**
    (¼ cup)
½   **cup dairy sour cream**
¼   **cup mayonnaise or salad dressing**
2   **tablespoons snipped fresh basil**
2   **tablespoons snipped fresh parsley**
1   **tablespoon milk**
    Fresh basil sprig (optional)

Nutrition information per serving: 331 calories, 14 g protein, 1 g carbohydrate, 30 g fat (8 g saturated), 51 mg cholesterol, 166 mg sodium.

Place whole heads of garlic in a small heavy saucepan with oil. Cook and stir over medium-low heat for 5 minutes. Cover; reduce heat to low for 15 minutes or until garlic is tender. Remove heads of garlic from oil; drain on paper towels. Cool.

Unroll pizza dough. Roll or stretch dough into a 15×10-inch rectangle; cut into six equal pieces. Transfer dough to a lightly greased 15×10×1-inch baking pan. Prick dough generously with a fork. Bake in a 425° oven for 7 to 8 minutes or until lightly browned.

Spread pesto over hot crusts. Arrange Brie or Camembert cheese slices atop pesto. Divide heads of garlic into cloves and peel. With a small, sharp knife, cut cloves lengthwise in half (small cloves can be left whole). Press garlic pieces into cheese. Bake pizzas for 8 to 10 minutes more or until cheese softens. To serve pizza, cut each piece in half diagonally.

Makes 12 servings.

2 **whole heads garlic**
¼ **cup olive oil or cooking oil**
1 **10-ounce package refrigerated pizza dough**
½ **cup purchased pesto**
8 **ounces cold Brie or Camembert cheese, cut into ⅛-inch-thick slices**

Nutrition information per serving: 243 calories, 8 g protein, 14 g carbohydrate, 17 g fat (1 g saturated), 20 mg cholesterol, 310 mg sodium.

Garlic, Brie, and Pesto Mini-Pizzas

Pizza
Margherita

This basil-scented pizza was invented and named for Italy's Queen Margherita, who reigned in the 1800s.

Prepare Pizza Dough. Grease an 11- to 13-inch pizza pan or baking sheet. On a lightly floured surface, roll half of the dough into a circle 1 inch larger than pizza pan. Transfer dough to pan. (Reserve remaining dough for another use.) Build up edges slightly. Prick generously with a fork. Do not let rise. Bake in a 425° oven for 10 to 12 minutes or until lightly browned.

Sprinkle mozzarella cheese over hot crust. Arrange tomato slices in a circular pattern atop cheese. Drizzle with oil. Sprinkle with fresh basil and Parmesan cheese.

Bake about 12 minutes more or until cheese melts and pizza is heated through.

Makes 12 servings.

Pizza Dough (see recipe, page 179)
1 **cup shredded mozzarella cheese (4 ounces)**
1 **ripe medium yellow tomato, thinly sliced**
1 **ripe medium red tomato, thinly sliced**
1 **tablespoon olive oil or cooking oil**
¼ **cup snipped fresh basil**
¼ **cup grated Parmesan cheese**

Nutrition information per serving: 167 calories, 6 g protein, 22 g carbohydrate, 6 g fat (2 g saturated), 7 mg cholesterol, 135 mg sodium.

Smoked Salmon and Chèvre Pizza

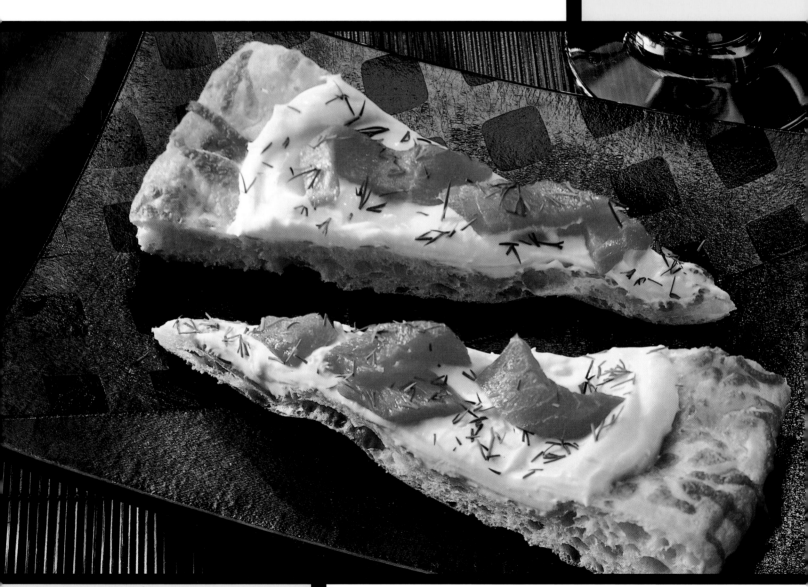

This trendsetting appetizer pizza offers an elegant start to a special-occasion dinner.

4 ounces soft goat cheese (chèvre)

2 tablespoons dairy sour cream

2 teaspoons prepared horseradish

1 16-ounce package Boboli (12-inch Italian bread shell)

3 ounces thinly sliced smoked salmon (lox-style), cut into ½-inch strips

1 tablespoon snipped fresh dill or 1 teaspoon dried dillweed

In a small mixing bowl combine goat cheese, sour cream, and horseradish. Mix well.

Place the bread shell on a lightly greased baking sheet. Spread goat cheese mixture evenly over the bread shell. Arrange salmon over goat cheese mixture. Sprinkle with dill.

Bake pizza in a 400° oven about 8 minutes or until hot.

Makes 12 servings.

Nutrition information per serving: 138 calories, 7 g protein, 17 g carbohydrate, 5 g fat (2 g saturated), 9 mg cholesterol, 299 mg sodium.

Stuffed Jalapeños

This recipe works equally well with Anaheim chili peppers. For best results, choose Anaheim peppers that are long and skinny.

In a small mixing bowl stir together cream cheese, green onion, pimiento, and garlic. Spoon mixture into pepper halves. Cover and chill until serving time.

Before serving Anaheim stuffed peppers, cut into 2-inch bite-size pieces.

Makes about 12 servings.

4 ounces soft-style cream cheese
2 tablespoons finely chopped
     green onion
2 tablespoons chopped pimiento,
     drained
1 clove garlic, minced
12 jalapeño chili peppers or 2 to
     3 Anaheim chili peppers, halved
     lengthwise and seeded

Nutrition information per serving: 42 calories, 1 g protein, 2 g carbohydrate, 3 g fat (2 g saturated), 10 mg cholesterol, 35 mg sodium.

For best results, choose a wheel of Brie that's fairly firm when you squeeze it gently.

Cut cheese into 8 wedges. Set aside. On a piece of waxed paper, a small plate, or a small mixing bowl, stir together flour and mustard. In another small mixing bowl stir together egg and milk. In another small mixing bowl stir together bread crumbs, red pepper, and black pepper.

Coat each piece of cheese in flour mixture. Dip into egg mixture and coat with bread crumb mixture. Dip again into egg mixture and then into bread crumb mixture.

Deep-fry coated cheese wedges in hot oil (365°) for 30 to 60 seconds or until golden brown. Drain on paper towels. Garnish with fresh herbs and serve warm with jelly.

Makes 8 servings.

1 **8-ounce round Brie or Camembert cheese, chilled**
2 **tablespoons all-purpose flour**
2 **teaspoons dry mustard**
1 **egg**
2 **tablespoons milk**
½ **cup fine dry bread crumbs**
¼ **teaspoon ground red pepper**
¼ **teaspoon ground black pepper**
   Oil for deep-fat frying
   Fresh herbs
½ **cup jalapeño or other pepper jelly, warmed**

Nutrition information per serving: 220 calories, 8 g protein, 19 g carbohydrate, 12 g fat (6 g saturated), 55 mg cholesterol, 239 mg sodium.

Fried Deviled Brie

Spread some of the pizza sauce on half of each tortilla. Sprinkle Monterey Jack cheese atop pizza sauce on each tortilla. Top with pepperoni and olives. Fold tortillas in half; press down edges gently.

In a large skillet or griddle cook tortillas, 2 or 3 at a time, over medium heat about 4 minutes or until cheese melts, turning once.

Cut each tortilla into three triangles.

Makes 9 servings.

½ cup pizza sauce
6 7-inch flour tortillas
2 cups shredded Monterey Jack cheese with
    jalapeño peppers or Monterey Jack cheese
    (8 ounces)
⅓ cup finely chopped pepperoni
3 tablespoons sliced pitted ripe olives

Nutrition information per serving: 194 calories, 9 g protein, 13 g carbohydrate, 12 g fat (6 g saturated), 27 mg cholesterol, 427 mg sodium.

Pizza Quesadillas

Crostini

These crisp slices of French bread are topped with a piquant tomato, olive, and chili pepper mixture. Be sure to drain the topping well to prevent the bread from becoming soggy.

In a medium mixing bowl stir together tomatoes, olives, onion, anchovy (if desired), vinegar, chili pepper, and garlic. Let stand at room temperature for 20 to 30 minutes.

Meanwhile, bias-slice the bread into ½-inch-thick slices. Place bread slices on a baking sheet.

Bake bread in a 350° oven about 5 minutes or until light brown. Turn bread over and bake 5 minutes more.

Evenly distribute mozzarella cheese slices over toasted bread. Drain tomato and olive mixture. Top slices with a spoonful of tomato and olive mixture.

Return bread slices to oven and bake for 5 minutes more or until cheese melts and tomato and olive mixture is heated through.

Makes about 20 crostini.

2 medium ripe tomatoes, peeled, seeded, and chopped (1 cup)

4 Calamata olives, pitted and chopped, or pitted ripe olives, chopped

¼ cup finely chopped red onion

1 canned anchovy fillet, drained, patted dry, and chopped (optional)

1 tablespoon balsamic or red wine vinegar

1 tablespoon finely chopped poblano chili pepper

1 large clove garlic, minced

1 8-ounce loaf baguette-style French bread

5 ounces mozzarella cheese, thinly sliced

Nutrition information per crostini: 54 calories, 3 g protein, 7 g carbohydrate, 2 g fat (1 g saturated), 4 mg cholesterol, 114 mg sodium.

In a medium mixing bowl combine avocados and lime juice. Using a potato masher, coarsely mash avocado mixture (mixture should be slightly lumpy).

Stir roasted sweet pepper, green onions, jalapeño or serrano peppers, salt, black pepper, and red pepper into avocado mixture. Cover and chill until serving time. Serve with tortilla chips.

Makes about 1⅔ cups.

*Note: To roast sweet red pepper, halve pepper and remove stem, membrane, and seeds. Place pepper, cut side down, on a foil-lined baking sheet. Bake in a 425° oven for 20 to 25 minutes or until skin is bubbly and black. Place pepper in a clean brown paper bag; seal and let stand for 20 to 30 minutes or until cool enough to handle. Pull the skin off gently and discard.

2   **medium avocados, seeded, peeled, and cut up**
1   **tablespoon lime juice**
1   **medium red sweet pepper, roasted and chopped,* or ½ cup chopped purchased roasted red pepper**
3   **green onions, finely chopped**
1   **to 2 tablespoons chopped jalapeño or serrano chili peppers**
¼   **teaspoon salt**
¼   **teaspoon ground black pepper**
⅛   **teaspoon ground red pepper**
    Tortilla chips

Nutrition information per tablespoon: 26 calories, 0 g protein, 2 g carbohydrate, 2 g fat (0 g saturated), 0 mg cholesterol, 21 mg sodium.

Gunpowder Guacamole

Index

Metric Cooking Hints

By making a few conversions, cooks in Australia, Canada, and the United Kingdom can use the recipes in *Better Homes and Gardens®* *Home for Dinner* with confidence. The charts on this page provide a guide for converting measurements from the U.S. customary system, which is used throughout this book, to the imperial and metric systems. There also is a conversion table for oven temperatures to accommodate the differences in oven calibrations.

Product Differences: Most of the ingredients called for in the recipes in this book are available in English-speaking countries. However, some are known by different names. Here are some common American ingredients and their possible counterparts:
- Sugar is granulated or castor sugar.
- Powdered sugar is icing sugar.
- All-purpose flour is plain household flour or white flour. When self-rising flour is used in place of all-purpose flour in a recipe that calls for leavening, omit the leavening agent (baking soda or baking powder) and salt.
- Light-colored corn syrup is golden syrup.
- Cornstarch is cornflour.
- Baking soda is bicarbonate of soda.
- Vanilla is vanilla essence.
- Green, red, or yellow sweet peppers are capsicums.
- Golden raisins are sultanas.

Volume and Weight: Americans traditionally use cup measures for liquid and solid ingredients. The chart, above right, shows the approximate imperial and metric equivalents. If you are accustomed to weighing solid ingredients, the following approximate equivalents will be helpful.
- 1 cup butter, castor sugar, or rice = 8 ounces = about 250 grams
- 1 cup flour = 4 ounces = about 125 grams
- 1 cup icing sugar = 5 ounces = about 150 grams

Spoon measures are used for smaller amounts of ingredients. Although the size of the tablespoon varies slightly in different countries, for practical purposes and for recipes in this book, a straight substitution is all that's necessary.

Measurements made using cups or spoons always should be level unless stated otherwise.

Useful Equivalents

⅛ teaspoon = 0.5 ml
¼ teaspoon = 1 ml
½ teaspoon = 2 ml
1 teaspoon = 5 ml
¼ cup = 2 fluid ounces = 50 ml
⅓ cup = 3 fluid ounces = 75 ml
½ cup = 4 fluid ounces = 125 ml

⅔ cup = 5 fluid ounces = 150 ml
¾ cup = 6 fluid ounces = 175 ml
1 cup = 8 fluid ounces = 250 ml
2 cups = 1 pint
2 pints = 1 liter
½ inch = 1 cm
1 inch = 2 cm

Baking Pan Size

American	Metric
8×1½-inch round baking pan	20×4-cm sandwich or cake tin
9×1½-inch round baking pan	23×3.5-cm sandwich or cake
11×7×1½-inch baking pan	28×18×4-cm baking pan
13×9×2-inch baking pan	32.5×23×5-cm baking pan
2-quart rectangular baking dish	30×19×5-cm baking pan
15×10×1-inch baking pan	38×25.5×2.5-cm baking pan (Swiss roll tin)
9-inch pie plate	22×4- or 23×4-cm pie plate
7- or 8-inch springform pan	18- or 20-cm springform or loose-bottom cake tin
9×5×3-inch loaf pan	23×13×6-cm or 2-pound narrow loaf pan or pâté tin
1½-quart casserole	1.5-liter casserole
2-quart casserole	2-liter casserole

Oven Temperature Equivalents

Fahrenheit Setting	Celsius Setting*	Gas Setting
300°F	150°C	Gas Mark 2
325°F	160°C	Gas Mark 3
350°F	180°C	Gas Mark 4
375°F	190°C	Gas Mark 5
400°F	200°C	Gas Mark 6
425°F	220°C	Gas Mark 7
450°F	230°C	Gas Mark 8
Broil		Grill

*Electric and gas ovens may be calibrated using Celsius. However, increase the Celsius setting 10 to 20 degrees when cooking above 160°C with an electric oven. For convection or forced-air ovens (gas or electric), lower the temperature setting 10°C when cooking at all heat levels.